FIVE GOOD REASONS *NOT* TO
SNARE A MILLIONAIRE

*You'll be able to get by with a smaller and less attractive wardrobe
*You won't have the extra expense of larger insurance policies to cover the expensive gifts you'll receive
*You won't have to worry so much about dieting since you won't be taken to nearly as many elegant restaurants
*You won't have to hassle with prenuptial agreements should you decide to marry
*There will be no threat of developing a taste for the finer things in life

D1267567

How To Snare A Millionaire

LISA JOHNSON

St. Martin's Paperbacks

HOW TO SNARE A MILLIONAIRE

Copyright © 1995 by Northwest Publishing, Inc.

All rights reserved. No part of this book may be used or reproduced in any manner whatsoever without written permission except in the case of brief quotations embodied in critical articles or reviews. For information address St. Martin's Press, 175 Fifth Avenue, New York, NY 10010.

ISBN: 0-312-96517-6

Printed in the United States of America

Northwest Publishing, Inc. edition published as *How to Date a Millionaire* 1995
St. Martin's Paperbacks edition/May 1998

10 9 8 7 6 5 4 3 2 1

Contents

O N E
Why Them? Why You? Why Me?

WHY DATE A MILLIONAIRE?

Some women would laugh and find the answer to this question ridiculously obvious. Others would scorn such a mercenary pursuit. To the latter, I say, "don't knock it until you try it, Toots." If you don't know why you should date a millionaire, let me give you five good reasons:

- It's fun! The wealthy can provide you with wonderful experiences free of financial worries.

- You deserve it! Every woman should have the opportunity to be pampered and spoiled at least a few times in her life. It's out there to be enjoyed. What makes anyone else more deserving than you?

- It will give you something to compare. Once you've tasted the cream, you might find you prefer the wholesomeness of skim milk, but you should at least have the opportunity to make a comparison.

- The experience can help you grow. New, positive situations can expand your horizons and make you a more content, interesting person.

- You'll derive satisfaction from it. "I came, I saw, I conquered, yawn." Until you know what you can conquer, you'll always wonder what you could have done, what you could have had. Why not try and see?

Now, in all fairness, there are some good reasons *not* to date a millionaire. They include:

- You'll never be accused of golddigging.

- You'll be able to stay comfortably within your own perimeters and won't have to venture out.
- You'll be able to get by with a smaller and less attractive wardrobe.
- You won't have the extra expense of larger insurance policies to cover the expensive gifts you'll receive.
- You won't have to worry so much about dieting since you won't be taken to nearly as many elegant restaurants.
- You won't have to concern yourself with competition from all those greedy, stop-at-nothing bimbos who throw themselves at men with money.
- You won't have to hassle with prenuptial agreements should you decide to marry.
- There will be no threat of developing a taste for the finer things in life.

Comparing the two lists, I'd say you might as well give it a try. You have far more to gain than you have to lose.

There are some who would say, "Why be dependent on a man for luxurious experiences? Go out, make your own millions, and provide those luxuries for yourself!" Well, I'm all for that if you can do it. I personally don't know how. I do know how to convince others to provide things for me, and I'm sharing that knowledge with you.

I've dated myriads of millionaires, and I'm not any worse for it. I don't believe I've been spoiled at all. As a matter of fact, I feel that because I know what it's like to attend elaborate balls and banquets, I can now honestly say I'm just as content hiking in the mountains. Because I know what it's like to receive expensive jewelry from men to whom money is no object, I can be just as grateful to a finance-conscious man who brings me a plant he lovingly grew himself. Because I have dated men on all levels of the economic spectrum, I can better identify the things that are truly valuable to me. Once you start dating millionaires, you'll see what I mean. It might surprise you to discover just what exactly is valuable to you. It might not be money, leisure, or prestige. But you'll never know until you try them.

No Guilt Allowed

Now, if you're feeling a little guilty just for browsing through these pages, don't worry about it. And don't believe for a second that by actually hunting them down and aiming at them, you'll be taking advantage of these poor, defenseless millionaires. My friend, by being an attractive, interesting companion, you'll be doing them a great favor!

Put yourself in their shoes. If you wanted to dine in your favorite restaurant then go to a Broadway opening, you certainly wouldn't want to do it alone, would you? You'd be grateful for an intriguing companion, right? I have season symphony tickets and I'm delighted when I find someone who enjoys symphony music as much as I do, and someone who behaves himself in public. I'm happy to have him come along, and I don't give the cost a second thought. Millionaires are the same way, only on a much more exalted scale. They often do interesting and exciting things, and many frantically search for someone wonderful to accompany them.

This book will give you some expert advice on how to become the wonderful woman a wealthy man would be ecstatic to have at his side. It will help you find a millionaire, captivate him, and maybe even marry him, if that's your desire.

And if that's not your desire, this book can also help you become a more interesting, comfortable, and confident person. Millionaires worth your while generally appreciate quality, and on the following pages, you'll learn how to incorporate quality into your very being. Read on. You have nothing to lose, and only excitement to gain.

You Asked For It

You might be asking yourself, "Who is this woman? Who does she think she is? Who died and made her the goddess of propriety? Why does she think she's qualified to tell me how to act? And how does she know so much about millionaires, if she's not one herself?" These are very good questions, and I have some very good answers.

To tell you the truth, it was not my idea to write this book in the first place. My friends implored me to do it.

It all started with a phone call from James, who just recently made his first million. Your first lesson is not to overlook these fresh types. James has season NBA tickets on the sixth row, center court. It's a great vantage point for seeing the games, and also for checking out other millionaires.

"L.A.," he said to me, "my secretary asked me what she needs to do to date a rich man, so I decided to call the expert and ask you."

That came as a surprise to me. I realized, of

course, that a rather large number of the men I date seem to be economically gifted, but I didn't think anyone else would notice. "Expert?" I stammered, the word sounded so crass and callous. "What makes you think I'm an expert?"

"Look at your roster," he replied. "You're seeing two millionaires at the moment, and over the years, you've dated more than I can count."

Every woman should have a few close male friends. James is one of mine, and, in true millionaire form, he is quite observant of things financial.

Of course I couldn't argue with him. Professional athletes, entertainers, businessmen, entrepreneurs, men of inherited wealth—they are all on my list. You'd probably recognize the names of many. But when James added them up and deemed me the expert on dating wealthy men, I was overcome with modesty. I don't think it was false.

"She can't be serious about wanting advice, can she?" I asked.

"You bet she does," he replied. "L.A., you ought to write a book."

An idea was born.

"But until you do," he continued, just give me a couple of quick tips I can toss at her. She's trying really hard. She'll be grateful for anything."

I reeled off the first two items that popped into my sarcastic little mind. "Tell her not to try too hard. She shouldn't bleach her hair, and she'd best stay away from over-sized silicone implants."

James burst out laughing. "L.A., you're not going to believe this, but I swear I'm serious. This week she came into the office with a new hair-color—platinum blond. And she's suddenly become what has to be a size-D, surgically enhanced. I asked her why the changes, and that's what got us started on the subject of dating millionaires. This is hilarious!"

It probably wasn't all that hilarious to his poor secretary, and I didn't find it too humorous either. I was saddened to realize that there are actually women out there who believe that a huge, jiggly chest and hair stripped of natural color will improve their chances with the economically elite. Perhaps a book on the subject could be useful. It might save these women from making expensive, tasteless mistakes.

I began asking my single friends if they would be interested in a book like this. They all agreed it was a fantastic idea, and begged to see advance copies of the manuscript. I even asked the opinions of a number of wealthy men, and the general consensus was that if it didn't teach women to be conniving and manipulative, they'd appreciate a guide. It could elevate some nice women from slatternly status and help them appreciate the same things that millionaires do. "It would be as if you were seeding the pond," said one outdoorsy type.

My research began from there. I discreetly talked to millionaires, to the women who date them, to their sisters, brothers, wives and parents. I read books on the subject, and made a long list of my own personal experiences. I began to see patterns and trends. Of course there are exceptions to every rule, but for the most part, the tenets I outline for you in this book hold up.

WHO AM I TO TELL YOU?

Before I go any farther, I want you to realize that I, personally, was born with a set of very average tools. I'm decent-looking but not striking, intelligent but not brilliant, interesting but not extraordinary. I've got a fair build, but my body would never be mistaken for a model's. I'm somewhat witty, but not exuberantly dazzling. And above all, I hardly come from a well-to-do family. Oh, my parents were middle-class comfortable, and we *were* rich in culture and love, but we were not considered particularly well-off. Let me assure you that if an average person like me can date a number of million-aires, you can too.

My background is very ordinary: I was raised in a somewhat small town by Southern California standards. My basically all-American upbringing included sports, music, church, lots of reading and writing, and the same traumas of breakouts and breakups that most of us share. My parents divorced and remarried. I attended a large, private, out-of-state university, and graduated early with honors, but my major was journalism, not nuclear physics, so it wasn't that difficult. I spent a few years studying and doing charity work abroad, then returned to the U.S. and settled into magazine and newspaper writing. I speak a second language. Really nothing outstanding there.

I've always had an active social life, and for reasons I'd never before examined, millionaires seem to like me. Not only do they date me, but as friends they take me into their confidence. They ask my advice on the women they date, on the clothes they wear, on the parties they give, on the events they attend. One even offered to pay me to line him up with attractive, upstanding women, and promised a bonus of several thousand dollars if the dates ended in marriage! He's still available, by the way. Anyone interested?

I've been proposed to by quite a number of millionaires. I've had more than 65 proposals in all, and some have been rescinded. But I've managed to elude serious commitment up to this point. I suppose I'll get around to it someday—when I find a man who can give me what I want, and can appreciate what I have to give.

I am currently living in the heart of a major U.S. city, in a comfortable condo I'm purchasing with the money I earn. I'll admit that some of the nicest things I own are gifts from my male friends, but I value the skiing snapshot taped to my refrigerator as much as I value the framed platinum record album hanging on my wall, and I treasure the over-sized tee-shirt as much as I love the diamond and amethyst jewelry.

I'm 30-ish and I keep blissfully busy with travel, writing and editing assignments, friends, family, charitable causes, and as much physical activity as I can get. I really don't believe I'm so different from most of you, and I'm about to erase more of our differences by sharing important information that might not have occurred to you at this point in time.

OUR LITTLE SECRET

You don't have to feel that just because you were

born in a lower socio-economic class, a man from the upper-crust is not on your menu. Don't think that if you weren't gifted with the looks of Cindy Crawford, you won't have a chance with a rich man. I like to think of myself as living proof that rather average people can captivate the wealthy, or anyone else they're interested in.

You're on the verge of developing and refining traits that are positively fatal to the elite. It all revolves around a simple little secret that I've finally been able to put my finger on:

Take what you have and cultivate it—expand it. Make the most out of what you've got. Live ethically. Listen. Learn. Reach. Obtain. Discard that which drags you down, incorporate that which sends you soaring. Then use what you've gained to support others. I've tried to do this all my life, and I've found it extremely effective. It's worked for me, enabling an average person to be sought-after by some very exceptional men. It can work for you too.

Let's start applying it.$

T W O
Looking Like A Million
From the Outside In

It's what's inside that really counts, but no one is going to discover all those wonderful things within you if they can't get past the outer shell. It's an unfortunate truth that looks are important.

Physical attraction is important to you, isn't it? Would you make any effort to get to know a greasy-haired man in a holey T-shirt and a half-unzipped fly? Painfully disgusting, no? His heart could be solid gold, but the outer wrapping would probably deter you from making much of an effort to get to know what's inside.

Millionaires are really not so different from you or me in this respect. They want to associate with people who are attractive to them. They're human. Surprise. Admittedly though, not all of them have truly refined taste when it comes to women's appearance. Many wealthy men won't be able to tell if that's your natural hair color, or if those are your real eyelashes. But, (and this is absolutely essential information for you to remember,) rich men are surrounded by women whose opinions count, and those women will know if you're a phony. Millionaires' mothers, sisters, ex-wives, and friends like me will know, and we'll be more than happy to pass along information and judgment. We are relentless in our drive to assure that the rich men close to us obtain the women they deserve, and not end up with greedy, plastic bimbos. It won't hurt to know how to pass our scrutiny. We can be consummately influential.

Also, let's face it—anyone can have large silicone implants, liposuction, hair-extensions, plastic surgery, colored contacts, etc., and many do. As a matter of fact, man-made women are a dime a dozen, and they're constantly throwing themselves at the feet of the wealthy. The wealthy, in turn, often find these types common, artificial, boring, passé. They prefer someone who is attractive on the outside, yes, but someone whose intrigue goes far deeper. You want to give a hint of that intrigue on the surface, but not try to push all your goodies in his face at once.

I still smile when I read a quote from a letter I received from a very dear, very rich man: "Right, you're not a *Playboy* centerfold with the giant casabas and the retouched face. You're better. You have a challenging mind, and a desire for progression in this life and for growth as an individual." Those words were followed by a marriage proposal.

Had I looked as if I were soliciting a little extra business on the side, this man would never have gotten to know anything about my inner worth. If you're a woman of kindness, integrity, passion, creativity, and intellect (and believe me, if you're not already, you can become one), you want it to show. Almost all men appreciate this—not just the wealthy.

So how do you let your stellar inner qualities show through? Not necessarily with the look of a raging super-model. As a matter of fact, most millionaires prefer a look that is far more conservative than you might guess. I had this point driven home one day when I was walking down the street and a prominent media personality approached me out of the blue. I was wearing a kelly green T-shirt, a navy blazer, a white denim skirt slightly above my knees, white socks, and Keds. (I was commuting and needed comfortable shoes.) My blond hair was hanging down my back, I was vaguely tanned, and after a full day's work, my makeup was somewhat faded. I certainly didn't feel beautiful. But as this man was driving by, he spotted me, pulled into the nearest parking lot, and walked up to me using the brilliant line, "Excuse me, but haven't we met before?" Recognizing him, I forgave him the cliché and we chatted for a while. Since I seldom give out my phone number on the first meeting, he gave me his card, and implored me to call. Later, after we'd dated several times, I asked him what had made him stop that day. "Just something about your look," he replied. "You looked clean, fresh, happy, a little playful."

DANGER SIGNS

Now there are some looks that will definitely send off the wrong signals. Millionaires are not interested in women who wouldn't be appropriate in their high-priced worlds, and they don't want a woman who looks like she could be purchased with a crumpled $20 bill on any street corner. Oh, they might flirt with the cheap and sleazy, but they're not going to take them to the kinds of places you want to go, and they're not going to get involved in quality relationships with them.

As examples, I give you the pro-athlete and rock star groupies. Those women with big hair and bustlines and short skirts and intellects can get the celebrities' attention for a few hours, but they're not the kinds of women rich men are going to take home to Mama, or to a fine restaurant.

There have been a myriad of movies made, *My Fair Lady*, *Pretty Woman*, and *Born Yesterday*, to name a few, that focus on taking women out of the gutter and into the ballroom, so to speak. Much of the difference has to do with character, but no small amount of emphasis is placed on achieving the appropriate look.

You definitely want an image that's refined and sophisticated, yet slightly sexy. I'll tell you how to achieve that look, no matter who you are. We'll start from the top of your perfectly coifed head and work our way down to the tip of your well-manicured toes.

Hair Apparent

First let's talk about color. The absolute perfect color for you is your natural one, perhaps with a few highlights and maybe with the gray streaks covered. Don't even toy with the idea of drastically dying it. Think of how startling it is to see Demi Moore and Julia Roberts as blondes. Don't you think they're much more attractive when they wear the natural color they were born with?

Your natural color is what matches your skin, brows, lashes, and everything else on your face and body. Of course it's fine to hide those gray hairs, but make sure you blend them in with your natural color. If you have dark hair, make it look rich and shiny with a henna rinse and a good conditioner. If you must toy with it, do it half a shade darker perhaps, or use burgundy highlights, but why would you ever dream of going blond? Most often you end up with that disgusting orangey-gold color. You know what I'm talking about—the stuff that looks like rusty water. Some beauticians have the nerve to call it honey blonde. I can't believe they actually take money for making women look that way.

Then there's the root problem. Unless you have your hair colored at least every three weeks (which is murder on your locks), you're going to have dark roots showing, and there's nothing tackier than that. Why bother with it? You'll be much less self-conscious, and freer to enjoy what's going on around you, if you just do the best you can with the color you have. Why suffer from more bad hair days than you have to?

Now for the style. There is one quick rule. Wear a cut that keeps things simple. Oh, it's fine to have your hair done up in an exotic way for a special occasion, but for everyday wear, keep it as simple and low-maintenance as possible. Unless you're a wealthy Dallas dowager who can get away with it, bigger is *not* better. All that teasing and spray do not make your hair look very user-friendly, if you know what I mean. They do not entice a man to run his fingers through your hair. They're also very inhibiting. Big hair does not sustain rides in convertibles or on Harleys (Harley Davidson motorcycles are essential status symbols these days), or walks in the rain. And should a millionaire invite you on a tropical vacation or up to a remote cabin for the weekend, big, elaborate hair will be a hassle, especially if you can't style it yourself, or if it takes you three hours and a lot of paraphernalia to do. Go for a softer, less-brazen look. It's far more elegant, and far more inviting.

Also, watch those perms and super-straightening processes. They can leave your hair looking fried, damaged, extremely unnatural. If you have naturally curly hair, put a palm-full of mousse in it for softness and shine, then revel in it! You're the envy of every straight-haired woman on the planet. Look at Cher. She has beautiful straight hair, but you see her most often photographed these days with a head-full of curls.

If you have straight hair and are not satisfied with letting it elegantly drape shiny and long, make sure that whatever you do to obtain curls is 100 percent safe and healthy. Don't scrimp by using unskilled hair-stylists or substandard perm products.

You might consider taking a look in your high school yearbook, and asking yourself if the style you're wearing today is similar to what you wore back then. If it is, it's probably time for a change. Just because it worked for you in the past does not mean it's working today. Look through magazines, see what you like, then save your money and make an appointment at a prestigious salon in your area. It will be expensive, but it will be worth it. Tell the stylist you want an easy care look that's not too extreme, but fairly vogue. While there, be friendly and warm to the other clients in the salon. Chances are, they'll be connected to a number of wealthy men. You could come out of the shop with a stunning new look, and some stunning new contacts.

Skin Deep

Be careful with your skin! No more basking in the sun for you—use self-tanning lotions, or a tanning salon if you absolutely must, to get that healthy bronzed look you may feel you need. The sun can and will make you look old before your time, so slather sunscreen on every day before you go out, and reapply it if you're outside for long.

It's much easier to take care now, before you age much, by keeping your face clean and by using high-quality (but not necessarily high priced) moisture lotions and sunscreens. Facelifts in later life are painful and harsh. That taut, smooth, stretched look works fine for drums, but it doesn't always go well on the human countenance. If you think plastic surgery will make you look that much better, think about it for a long time, and consult several physicians, then if it will really make a difference, do it. But try to avoid wrinkling in the first place.

Your complexion should look clean, healthy,

glowing. Smoking can muddy your complexion, as can foundation that is too thick or the wrong color. Ask a beauty consultant for advice on what looks best with your skin, and then check it in a number of different lighting situations. Keep your skin as soft and smooth as possible. It helps if you pamper your skin, and while you're doing that, don't forget to take care of your neck and hands as well. That's where many people look to discern a woman's age.

ALL EARS

I shouldn't have to write this, but there's something I think we all catch ourselves doing subconsciously every now and then, and it has to stop. *Do not stick your fingers in your ears and clean them in public.* I have a very refined friend whom I've often caught inserting her beautifully manicured fingers into her ears, scratching vigorously, then pulling her fingers out and examining what she found in there. I won't tell you what she does with it after that, but it's really quite disgusting. Keep your ears free of debris by cleaning them with a cotton swab or a tissue—make it part of your daily routine at home, in the privacy of your own bathroom. Don't pick at your ears in public. Don't even stick your fingers in your ears to scratch in public. Your gestures might be misunderstood. Was it a scratch or a pick? As you read this, you've probably inserted a finger in your ear right now, haven't you? Fingers off, earrings on.

Earrings can be wonderful and fascinating, if not overdone. Thank heavens those shoulder-duster apparatuses are no longer available, although you can still find a few in the reduced bins of your local super-discount mart. Resist the urge to buy them. Once again, subtle and refined is better than loud and brash, although some big earrings can be fun if they're the only major jewelry worn. You usually have to be rather tall to carry off the larger earrings well. Select a shape that suits your face. If you have fat cheeks like mine, never wear perfectly round earrings, but select those that are longer than they are wide. If you have a long face, round ones will do nicely.

Every woman should have at least one pair of authentic, truly elegant earrings. If you don't, look in your mother's or your grandmother's jewelry boxes, and see if they have any interesting gold or pearls that they don't wear and wouldn't mind passing along to you. It's better to have one really nice pair that goes with everything than hundreds of cheap pairs. Besides, if a millionaire you're seeing notes you wear the same earrings constantly, it is not unlikely he will give you another nice pair as a gift. I've collected my favorite and most valuable earrings this way. Men usually have a hard time knowing what to buy for you, and this will make it easier for them.

Also, make sure the metal on your earrings matches the metal on the rest of your jewelry and belt buckle too, if you can swing it. Gold with gold, silver with silver, bronze with bronze, etc. Minute details can make a difference.

Private Eyes

If the eyes are the mirrors to your soul, you don't want those mirrors overwhelmed by gaudy frames. Use colors that would naturally be found on your skin. I can't imagine whatever possessed anyone to come up with turquoise and emerald green eyeliners, eyeshadows, and mascaras. Those colors do not enhance your natural eye color, but call attention away from it. They look cartoonish. If you have a make-over at one of the more expensive makeup counters or salons (which I highly suggest), they'll never let those colors near you. A very deep, mossy green perhaps, and maybe a dark, dark navy, but nothing bright. And you won't find them heavily lining your eyes all the way around, either. You're not trying to make your eyes look like a Picasso painting, you're trying to accent them. The eyes, lashes, and brows are what should be noticeable, not the colors or lines on them.

And speaking of brows, no matter what happens to be trendy at the moment, do not pluck them into tiny little lines ala Lucy Ricardo. No one's eyebrows grow like that naturally, and an artificial, tweezed look is not what you want. However, if your eyebrows are rather bushy and tend to lunge toward each other across your forehead, you'll want to try plucking, or better still, waxing to separate them.

Also, be sure that you don't "lash out" by wearing over-extended false eyelashes, too many coats of mascara, or unnatural colors of the same product. It's best to avoid false eyelashes all together if that's possible. Try using a few coats of mascara, and separating those lashes when they stick together. Some people have their eyelashes dyed, which is a nice look, but can be damaging and painful. If you go for this process, make sure the technician tests it on you first. The best policy for eyelashes, like with everything else, is to keep them sweet and simple.

CHEEK CHECK

It's called "blush" for a good reason. You should apply it to your face to subtly define your cheeks and give them a healthy glow. Avoid making it look as if someone just slapped you, or scrubbed your face with strawberry Kool-Aid. The color you want to wear is the color your cheeks turn when you press your hand against them for a moment. Blend your blush well. If you can see where the color begins and ends, you need to work on it a little more. Once again, a visit to a fine makeup counter would help. If you're willing to purchase any little item from their line, a sales rep will usually give you application tips free of charge.

KNOW YOUR NOSE

You probably dislike your nose. Join the club. Most people are uncomfortable with their noses. But rest assured that you are your nose's own worst critic. You are the only one who even notices that it's slightly crooked, has a vague bump, or that one nostril is larger than the other. Stop worrying about it.

Oh, you can have plastic surgery if you can

afford it and your nose really obsesses you. If it makes you feel better about yourself, why not? But then again, why? A makeup specialist can show you a few tricks about shading, but for the most part, unless it has hair growing under it or out of it, (and I'd advise you to lose that quickly), there's not much you really need to do with your nose except smell and nuzzle. Don't turn it up, don't pick it, don't snort—these things go without saying. Accept your nose as an important, beautiful part of your individuality, and go on.

THE MOUTH THAT SCORES

Your mouth can be one of your most enticing features. Let's divide this into several parts. Lips first. What an intriguing part of your face your lips can be! Don't feel you have to follow whatever the current fashion may be—dying, silicone injecting, even tattooing. But keep your lips in good condition. You might want to apply a lip conditioner to them before you go to bed at night, or under your lipstick in the morning—it will reduce those tiny wrinkles and keep your lips from cracking.

If you're wearing a strong color, you should use lip liner to help prevent the lipstick from smearing and bleeding. This is the one part of your face where you can get away with colors that are somewhat brighter than natural. A deep or bright red can be striking. Burgundies, corals, pinks, and even browns can look fantastic. Try your best to match the color of your lips with the color of your fingernails, although this is not always essential. And avoid bright oranges, whites, pearlized looks, and candy pinks. Those colors seem either painfully trendy or just plain cheap to the millionaire.

Always carry a mirror with you when you wear lipstick, so you can touch it up. Nothing looks worse or less inviting than patchy lips, or lipstick streaks on the gleaming white enamel of your teeth. If you don't have a mirror and extra lipstick with you, when you start to feel the color blotch or bead, wipe it all off.

Oh, and be careful of the white residue that sometimes collects around the sides of your mouth when your lip protector starts to wear off. This is especially a problem for me when I ski. When I think about it, I carry a tissue and lip balm in my pocket, and use them after every other run. When I don't think about it, I look like I drink a big glass of milk after every other run. Not a pretty sight.

Teeth can be a dead class giveaway. Wealthy

people, and people who associate with wealthy people, do not have crooked, yellow, or broken teeth. Most of them had the money to wear tons of hardware on their mouths when they were young, and if not, they've had their teeth straightened, enameled, and whitened since.

If you should have had braces when you were little, I'd advise you to get them now. There's a good chance your employer's health plan will pay for most of it, but even if it doesn't, it's a very worthwhile investment. You don't even have to put off your pursuit of a millionaire while you're wearing those corrective devices—they can be rather interesting conversation pieces. Besides, these days your smile can almost always be corrected in little more than a year. As strange as it may sound, your dentist can probably do more to help your face than a plastic surgeon can.

You should visit your dentist at least once a year to have your teeth cleaned and examined. If your insurance will cover it, go to a prominent dentist in an exclusive neighborhood. You never know who you might meet in the waiting room. In addition, the doctor can recommend whiteners, and any other process you might want to try to get those teeth looking pearly and straight. Don't skimp on your teeth. Take the best care of them.

Now, we can't forget to mention breath. Don't think you can tell if your breath is good or bad by blowing into your cupped palm. Your nose has already accustomed itself to the odor of your breath, and will probably deceive you. After you eat, assume that your breath needs help, and do something about it. It's really not good taste to slip into the ladies room and work up a lather with the brush and paste you carry in your evening bag, so you'll probably want to carry breath mints with you.

Don't use gum. Chewing it, especially chewing it loudly, which most people do without thinking, is one of the most classless habits you can acquire. Just recently, at the Governor's Gala, I saw a large pink bubble emerge from the lips of a very elegantly dressed woman. It spoiled the whole effect. If you must chew gum, chew it while you're alone, and dispose of it where no one will ever see it or find it. Believe me, your friends will thank you for it.

WORST ENEMY/BEST FRIEND

Important—The worst enemy of your face and body is a cigarette. Smoke can damage the capillaries in your skin, and make you look old and hard before your time.

Smokers wrinkle. It's a fact. Cigarettes also have a nasty odor, stain your teeth and fingers yellow, and demonstrate that you have a general unconcern for your health. I cannot tell you how many men have said to me, "if she's a smoker, no matter what else she is, I don't want her."

Would you want someone defiling your expensive house or car, or ruining an elegant meal with a foul odor? Neither does the rich man, unless he smokes himself. Most do not. They're often too health conscious for that, and if not, perhaps the two of you can wrinkle and die young together.

If you're smoking, quit right now. Use nicotine patches if you must. They might seem expensive at first, but they'll probably cost less than the cigarettes you've been buying. Then save your cigarette money for a while and buy yourself a pair of nice earrings. If you want to look and feel your best, DO NOT SMOKE.

The best friend of your face is a smile. You look and feel your best while you're smiling. Just try and be upset or negative while your lips are curled heavenward. You're far more approachable and inviting when you appear happy.

I have a little trick I play on myself the morning after a truly horrendous night. I may feel like absolute fertilizer inside, and I may think I've never looked uglier, but I give myself a huge smile in the mirror right before I walk out the door, and I keep that smile on my face all the way to work. By the time I get to the office, I realize that things can't possibly be as bad as they seemed, because people are throwing happy, positive looks my way. I smile at them, they smile at me—it's a chain reaction.

BODY BUILDING

Perfect proportions are not essential, but being as close to your ideal weight as is possible *is*. Most men, wealthy or not, do not appreciate women who are overweight. Take a look in any paper that runs singles ads. Almost every ad specifies that the ideal person is "thin," "trim," or "not calorically challenged." Granted, most wealthy men do not seek partners in the classified section, but weight-obsession seems to cross economic boundaries.

Now there are many overweight women who are currently connected with very wealthy and powerful men, but you can bet the women were slender when they dated and married their husbands, and since then they've probably borne a child or two. These women can afford to be overweight. The rest of us cannot, for the sake of our own personal health and self-esteem, as well as for the sakes of the men who are concerned with those things.

If you're not overweight now but have a tendency toward it (that tendency is often discovered by looking at your mother), develop habits that will keep that weight off.

If you are overweight now, do whatever it takes to safely get rid of those extra pounds and make them stay away. Don't waste valuable time and money on fad diets, liquid diets, etc. They may be responsible for dramatic weight-loss in the beginning, but they almost never give lasting results. Observe what happened to Oprah Winfrey after she went off her much-publicized liquid diet. For all her slaving and suffering, she put most of her weight right back on in a number of weeks. Oprah, however, is an anomaly. Because of her powerful persona, she can carry her weight well. Most of the rest of us can't.

It's far safer and wiser to change your eating habits. Cut back on the fats and sugars. Eat more fresh fruit and vegetables, whole grains. Drink lots of water—plain water, perhaps with a lemon slice, but no carbonation or flavoring. Water will cut your appetite, and it's great for your system.

Also, you'll want to adjust your feelings about food. Food is not your friend, it is merely something you take into your system to sustain you. Of course, you can enjoy it, but it should not pacify or comfort you, and it certainly should not have a major influence in your life.

In addition, you'll want to get in the habit of being physically active. Walk more. If you need to go five or fewer blocks, walk, don't drive. If you need to use fewer than five flights of stairs, don't you dare take the elevator, especially if it's down a few floors. Don't you just abhor the person who stops the busy elevator merely to go down one floor?

Make it a goal to be involved in at least one very physically strenuous activity per week (hiking, skiing, tennis, swimming, biking, etc.), and try to indulge in some exercise every day—at least 20 minutes' worth. If the only thing that will get you motivated to move is investing a lot of money in aerobics classes, spa memberships, or fitness equipment, do it. Or perhaps make it a joint project with a friend so you can encourage each other. Do whatever it takes to make the heart pump and the muscles firm.

I live in a climate where outdoor activity is not always convenient, so, in addition to the racquetball courts and the workout facilities my condominium complex provides, I have a NordicTrack in my bedroom. I use it almost every day. Sometimes I use it early in the morning when I first get up, sometimes I use it when I get home from work while I watch the news. The machine was a gift from one of my wealthy friends, probably the most practical thing I've ever received. If I don't have time to get dressed up for the spa or even for the downstairs workout room, I can always grab a few minutes on the NordicTrack, wearing or not wearing whatever I like.

I enjoy this machine because it gives my upper body as well as my lower body a workout at the same time, and keeps me in shape for just about any physical activity in which I care to participate. Now, there are other exercise machines that can give you a great workout and keep you in top condition, and I strongly suggest you buy something along these lines. Consider it an investment in making yourself feel good. When you're in the best shape you can be, you'll be more confident, you'll have more stamina, and you won't feel those 21-year-old hard-bodied women have any advantages over you. They won't.

Following these guidelines, I've even gotten to the point where I often have to make an effort not to out-distance the men I date when we're involved in sports. Many older men, whom I find fascinating, have a hard time keeping up with me on the ski slopes or the mountain trails, so I'll reduce my speed a bit. This is not a concession to the male ego, but consideration to another human being. I know I don't like it when my date laughs as he breezes past me and leaves me in the dust—it makes me feel weak and foolish. I don't want to make anyone else feel that way, either. I *do* want them to feel, however, that they're with a vital person who values her body and takes care of it. You can make them feel that way too.

NAILING IT

Average, unpolished, dull nails often go unobserved by men, but beautiful, long, graceful nails are always noticed and appreciated. Keep your nails well-manicured if it's at all possible. You might want silk or enamel applications on them, but find a manicurist who can apply them with a natural look, who will not make them too long, nor will she square them off. Nails that are too long scare men and appear impractical. Nails that are rectangular make your fingers look blunt and clunky, no matter how long they are.

You won't see the best-dressed women wearing those styles. You also won't see them wearing bright orange or pearlized polish, or cute little decals or paintings on each finger. One decal might work every once in a while in a novelty situation, but for the most part, unless you're an Olympic track star, avoid an abundance of stripes, flowers, words, Santas, palm trees, etc.

Since you won't want to change your polish every day to match your outfit, select a color that will go with many different outfits, or use clear. And if you do wear color, make sure you keep it up. Stay on top of those chips and cracks. See your manicurist as often as you must. Nothing can look more alluring than beautiful nails elegantly poised on a long-stemmed crystal glass, across a candle-lit table. Wealthy men say it's exquisitely exciting. They like to imagine those beautiful hands poised in more intimate places. I've had more men than I can count comment favorably, almost lustfully, on my hands when my nails are well-manicured.

CROWNING JEWELS

You don't have to spend thousands of dollars on jewelry to look as though you're at home with the uppercrust. Too many jewels, even if they're authentic, are considered crass and tasteless. All your jewelry doesn't even have to be authentic—you can get away with rhinestones and zirconia if you don't overdo them. The secret to dressing well is not to overdo anything. Don't mix metals. Wear all gold, all silver, all copper, whatever. Pearls usually work for formal occasions—they're very subtle and elegant. When it comes to jewelry, try to avoid looking like you just ditched your sugar daddy or soaked your ex-husband, even if you did.

Sometimes one very interesting piece of jewelry, like a broach or a watch, can be a fun conversation starter. One day when I was strolling through Soho, I purchased a pin that looks like a clock with a little man dashing around the face. I sometimes attach it to a hat or a blazer lapel when I'm going to a party, and it piques people's interest. It would be tacky if I had the matching earrings and necklace, however, or if I wore it to the opera.

Beautiful ethnic jewelry can also work well, and it's not always expensive. If you're going out of the country, pick some up, or give a traveling friend some money and ask him or her to get some baubles for you. Some of the most arresting jewelry I own was purchased for me by friends vacationing in Paris and Kenya. People usually don't mind bringing you jewelry since it's often sold on the street, it's easy to find, and it doesn't take up a lot of space in their luggage.

THE SCENT OF A WOMAN

This is consummately important but frequently overlooked. The sense of smell should never be underestimated. The movie *The Scent of a Woman*, emphasized the fact that the memory of a woman's smell alone could be enough to keep a man going.

I remember getting a very late-night call from a famous musician, several hours after I'd left him for the evening. "I can still smell your scent on my hands, on my clothes," he said. "It is driving me mad." Another wealthy attorney called early the morning after a date to tell me that he'd smelled my perfume in his expensive sports car on his way to the office, and wanted to know if I was free for lunch. It wasn't the way I looked, tasted, or felt. It was my scent that had captivated these men. You can have the same effect.

My advice to you would be to pick two pleasant but unusual fragrances, one heavier for evening, one lighter for day, and make them your own—your signature scents, your trademarks. When people smell them, they will think of you.

I use Donna Karan at night, and Chanel Number 19 during the day. I usually carry a little vial of each in my purse, and I'm not above secretly spraying a little on the pillow or in the car of my homme du jour when he's otherwise occupied, so a part of my presence will remain long after I've left. Also, before a special evening, I'll take a nice hot bath using these fragrances' soaps or gels, slather on the matching lotion, and sprinkle my skin with the corresponding powder. It makes me feel pampered, and it makes the scent last much longer.

Now the scents you choose obviously can't be too common. If everyone is wearing them, they will not be uniquely yours. Nor can they be too strong. Some of the heavier perfumes are made with industrial strength ingredients—the kinds used in cleansers, floor waxes, and detergents. There is nothing subtle or intriguing about the woman you can smell coming a block away.

Also, what smells wonderful on your best friend may not be quite so nice when mixed with your own body chemistry, so make sure you try the scents on for several hours before you make a purchase. By the way, if your millionaire friend becomes infatuated with your scent, you can expect to receive some from him as a gift. It's another easy thing for him to pick up, and he's assured you'll like and use it.

A CLOTHES CALL

This is a difficult area to coach because individual style is very important. You don't want to be a clone of the Eastern Seaboard old money set, but you don't want to look like you just came from a costume party, either.

If you desire the elegant-yet-sexy look to which most wealthy men are attracted, you can easily go to any of the nicer department stores in your area and pick a wardrobe from the current Donna Karan collection, but that's not at all practical. Not only are those clothes rather expensive, but you'll look like every other woman at every event you attend. It wouldn't hurt, however, to study those looks in stores and in magazines, then adapt them to your own style. There are some things, however, that you should always take into consideration.

Texture is one of those things. So many people fail to place due importance on the sense of touch. Your clothes should not only look good, but *feel* good as well. Suede, silk, velvet—these fabrics, and others, feel good. They're comfortable for you to wear, and they make people want to softly touch you. When they do, it can be a sensual delight for both of you. Pay attention to how your clothes feel, and how they look like they feel.

Also pay attention to fabric. Natural fibers are the ones of choice, even if manmade fabrics are more practical. The wealthy wear mostly cotton, wool, silk, and linen, and so should you. In the long run, these fabrics usually wear better anyway, even if they are high maintenance. You might have to spend extra time and money pressing and dry-cleaning (rich people have other people take care of these chores for them), but many people consider natural fibers a sign of quality and taste.

See that your clothes are immaculate. If there's a stain on something or it's missing a button, don't wear it until you've fixed the situation. *Never* use safety pins, masking tape, or staples to hold anything together. They will always show somehow, and you're asking for embarrassment. A good rule to follow is, when in doubt, do without. It's better to wear something else.

Now let's move on to some individual articles of clothing:

DRESSES

A woman in a skirt generally calls more attention than a woman in pants, if for no other reason than it emphasizes the difference between the sexes. I found that out for myself, when, as an eager young reporter, I wore a skirt out to one of my first assignments, which was interviewing a couple of players at the Los Angeles Raiders training facility. There were many sports writers there, but I was the only one showing any leg, and I was also the only one getting any masculine attention. It was embarrassing, really, but it got me a number of dates and taught me a lesson. Under the circumstances, a dress probably wasn't appropriate, but in the right situation, it can be a powerful asset.

One of your biggest boons can be the little black dress. There is nothing so versatile and so flattering. It can be dressed up or down for day or night wear, and looks great on everyone, no matter how old they are. I have a gorgeous picture of my divorced mother, smiling proudly in her little black dress. I give copies of it to my friends to show to their wealthy divorced fathers. That picture has never failed to get a response.

When it comes to dress length, there are only two that I would advise against. The first is so dangerously short that very little stands between you and embarrassment, and the second is that stodgy, just-below the knee length that is favored by older British royalty, grandmothers, and politicians' wives.

Many people consider this classic, but you'll find classically dull is a more appropriate description. Most of these women are connected with wealthy men, but those wealthy men are notoriously connected with other women as well.

Dresses that are too tight or too low-cut are tacky. Some women think they're provocative, and they are—they provoke men into thinking that the woman wearing them can easily be had. This is not the impression you want to give a millionaire. Besides, these kinds of dresses are uncomfortable. You don't want to be consumed with the concern that something will pop out or fall off, do you? Why not relax? Besides, the wealthy generally make the assumption that if you're trying too hard to flaunt your physical virtues, you're probably compensating for a lack of other, more substantial assets.

But on the other hand, you don't want to wear dresses, or any other form of apparel, that are baggy and shapeless. Men and women of taste abhor the tent look. It looks careless, lazy, and usually wrinkled. Your body has variety and charm. Why hide it?

COLORS

When in doubt, wear black. You might not want it next to your face, but black is intriguing, and you can seldom go wrong with it. From black jeans to a black formal, it's almost always elegant, sexy and appropriate. Of course you have to know how to accessorize it—a splash of bright color or striking metal jewelry help, but know that black will work almost anywhere, any season, day or night. Color consultants will tell some of you stay away from it, but accessorize away their warnings then ignore them.

You don't need to hire an expensive color consultant to find out what looks best on you. All it really takes is a friend, a store, and a mirror. Grab blouses from a rack and hold them up to you. It should be obvious what works. There are a few magical colors that look fantastic on everyone—among them are turquoise blue, periwinkle, and fuchsia, their specific shades varying according to your complexion.

I remember sitting in a popular restaurant with a red-haired friend who was wearing a turquoise sweater. Now, Susie is an attractive woman, but I'd never before seen her get so much attention. Men we'd never met approached our table to get her name and number. I noticed several irritated women nudge their dates to keep them from staring. Everyone we spoke with commented on how wonderful Susie's eyes looked with that sweater. It was 'the' color, we agreed. It wouldn't hurt you to find clothes that have that effect. And don't buy things in colors that you are only marginally happy with. Just get the ones that make you feel special.

PANTS

There are a few cardinal rules when it comes to pants. Don't wear any made of that coarse polyester. Don't let your underwear lines show through, but *do* wear underwear with them if there's even the remotest chance of detection. You do not want people speculating about your lack of lingerie.

You can get away with almost any length of pants these days, unless they drag on the ground and become frayed, or unless they're so short your cheeks peek out. However, you should avoid long pants that show leg above your socks when you sit down (If you like the pants, consider purchasing longer socks.) Also, know that very short shorts are never appropriate in most affluent circles—not even in athletic venues. I recently attended a wedding reception where the guests couldn't help but notice a long-legged woman dressed in white "hot pants," navy stockings, and navy spike heels. While she had great legs, no one seemed to notice, and she became the object of much behind-the-back derision. She'd made a very unfortunate choice.

Be very careful when you buy pants. Look at them from the back and front. Notice what kinds of lines they create. Do they accentuate your tush? Your thighs? Your hips? Are they comfortable? You might want to get someone else's opinion (and not a salesperson's) before you purchase them. Another person can see your body from a different perspective.

STOCKINGS

You're going to find this hard to swallow, but even in this day and age, your ankles can make or break you. You don't believe me? Watch the response of a wealthy man to a woman whose leg hair pokes through her stockings, to a woman who wears baggy white socks with a skirt, or to a woman with an obvious run creeping out of her shoe. On the other hand, watch that same man's response to a woman with sheer black stockings stretching forth from a slit in a skirt. You feel better about yourself when your legs look long and sleek. Don't wear stockings or socks that detract from that.

Probably my biggest personal clothing weakness is brightly patterned stockings in loud colors. I love to wear them with solid colored dresses. But the men in my life make it no secret that they detest those tights, and the women think they're obnoxious too. Perhaps I should listen to them and leave the wild stockings in my drawer.

There is one other legwear fashion faux pas that you should *never* commit—it will betray you as a style derelict every time. Do not, I repeat, do not, wear shear stockings with jeans or with athletic shoes. Believe me, it looks lowly. Wear cotton or wool socks. Just take my word for it.

LINGERIE

Just because people don't normally see your underwear (and you should avoid styles that show it), doesn't mean you can skimp here. If you feel attractive on the inside, you'll feel attractive on the outside. And you're seldom more attractive than you feel.

It just doesn't work to slip a silk dress on over faded cotton panties and a bunchy graying bra. When it comes to underclothes, pamper yourself, regardless of whether your date is going to see them or not. Silky fabrics feel so good next to your skin, and just knowing that under your cotton blouse and khakis you're wearing a lacy teddy will give you a playful confidence you never knew you could have. For the fun of it someday, try wearing to work a garter belt and matching stockings under your clothes, so no one will see them. Your little secret will keep a smile on your face all day long.

Or consider this—try no underwear at all, if you're absolutely positive your secret will be safe. It will make you feel deliciously flirtatious and sexy. That's a ploy Marilyn Monroe frequently used. I know this because I have a wonderful aunt who used to work in the wardrobe department of a major movie studio. She said she and her co-workers would cringe when they saw Marilyn Monroe walking their way, because they knew she was coming to borrow something from their department that she could wear out on the street that day, and they knew she'd refuse to wear underwear with it. They pleaded with her. They begged. But she told them tight clothes were essential and visible panty lines catastrophic, so off she'd go, sans panties. The costumers may not have enjoyed indulging her, but numerous wealthy and powerful men did. Under the right circumstances, little or no underwear can go a long way. Just give it a try. Men have told me they find the thought of this extremely erotic, and so will you.

Make sure your bras and underwear match, and

see that they're immaculate. Contrary to what your mother told you, you'll probably never get in an accident and be embarrassed by the ambulance driver, but you should try to feel "good all under" for your own satisfaction, if not for anyone else's.

SHOES

Hopefully, you know when to wear dress pumps and when to wear tennies. Just as you wouldn't wear tennies with an evening dress, don't wear dressy high heels with jeans. That's a fairly common, yet fairly grave, fashion don't. On the whole, high heels with dresses tend to make your legs look more shapely and graceful, but stay away from those frighteningly tall and thin stiletto heels. My friend Daphne, a millionaire herself, calls them C.F.M.P.s, the last letter standing for pump, the rest you can figure out for yourself.

Take care that your shoes are always in good condition, that the heels aren't worn or scuffed. Try kicking off your good shoes before you start driving, or they'll have ugly scars on the backs. Above all, make sure your shoes are comfortable. Nothing looks worse than a woman hobbling down the street with a grimace on her face because her shoes are rubbing her feet raw.

I love to walk, and I revel in comfortable shoes. I was particularly grateful for them the day I happened to meet one of my wealthy male friends as I was strolling home from work. "I'll take you to dinner," he said as he sidled up to me.

"Fine," I replied. "First let me drop off this bulky briefcase." Dale followed me up to my condo, and as soon as I sat down to relax for a moment, Dale was on his knees, removing my shoes, and massaging my feet. I admit I felt a little awkward, but not half as awkward as I would have felt if I would have had huge blisters, calluses, and a nasty smell from shoes that were cheap or too-tight. You just never know.

LIVING PROOF

Are you getting the idea? You don't have to look as if you popped off the pages of a Ralph Lauren ad to attract a millionaire's eye. Your own personal, elegant style with a touch of the exotic will do quite well. It's that harsh look you want to avoid.

If you want to see proof of this, go to a popular club one night, and observe those around you—who is getting attention from whom. I had an experience the other night that will show you exactly what I mean.

The evening was winding down at a trendy club which many of the professional athletes in my area frequent, and I was feeling quite satisfied. I was comfortable in my form-fitting black dress with an abundance of silver jewelry, and I had in my matching bag the business cards of two very prominent and exciting bachelors. (I seldom give out my own phone number when asked, but I request the gentleman's card instead. That way I can check him out before I undertake to spend any time alone with them. Besides, I believe in letting men wait by the phone for *my* call. My days of dangling are long past.)

It was evident, however, that not every woman in the room was feeling as content as I was. I saw one particularly downcast sister, and I excused myself from the man who was escorting me to my car, to chat with her for a second.

She was wearing what looked like a pink puff-sleeve bikini top and a blue, ruffled mini-skirt with suspenders. She had on pink, spike-heeled ankle boots and ruffled socks to match. Her bangs reached for the stars, and her rainbow-colored eye makeup would have made Henri Matisse proud.

"That's some outfit," I told her, consolingly. "Did it help you meet anyone interesting tonight?"

"Nah," she responded dejectedly. "It's brand

new, and all it got me was groped by a waiter."

I'm going to carry a copy of this book around with me, in hopes of meeting this woman again some day. I will autograph it for her, and dog-ear the page that contains the following list.

I surveyed men of taste on what particularly excited them about a woman's looks, and what decidedly disgusted them. Their answers both amused and surprised me. Hands down, the things men most liked to see a woman wearing were the gifts they'd given her. Here are the rest of the results:

LOOKS THAT MAKE
ELEGANT MEN SALIVATE

Creamy white silk or satin on a dark-skinned woman

Bare shoulders on a warm summer night

Bare back on a warm summer night

A long string of pearls

Shorts, a chambray shirt, and white tennis shoes with hair pulled back in a ponytail

Looks that are crisp and clean

Gleaming white cotton blouses—especially with jeans

Black stockings

Lace-topped stockings (not panty hose)

Navy blazers

Fingernail polish

Suits with shorter skirts

Hair ribbons

The Grace Kelly style, i.e.. cardigans over crew-
neck sweaters

The Ralph Lauren look

Silk blouses

Creative clothes that aren't brassy

The basic black dress

Long hair

Soft fabrics

Light, summer dresses

Slingback pumps

A wee bit o' cleavage

Dark glasses

Long, form-fitting skirts

Outfits of two striking colors, such as copper and
black, olive and purple, etc.

Jeans with elegant leather boots

Anything chamois-colored

Shorter skirts with high heels

Berets

Silk suits

Silk warm-up suits

Lace body suits (underneath something else)

Luxurious lingerie

Camisoles and tap pants

Lacey teddies (but not red)

Men's boxer-type shorts made of a feminine material

"My shirts"

LOOKS THAT MAKE
ELEGANT MEN CRINGE

Skin tight leggings on out-of-shape women

Sloppy sweats in public

Wild-patterned stockings

Too much makeup

Heavy, bright-colored eyeliner

Dirty hair

Spiky hair

Tentlike jumpers (unless you're pregnant)

Big lace collars

Shorts with high-heels

Shorts with cowboy boots

Bell-bottom pants

Rabbit jackets (or anything else with rabbit fur)

Hip boots

Sweatshirts decorated with glitter and faux jewels

Tight leather suits

The grunge look

Lumpy bras under tight sweaters or t-shirts

Embarrassingly tight t-shirts

Hairy armpits

Hairy legs

Bra straps showing

Big, ruffled collars

Brown leather shoes with bright-colored silky dresses

Scuffed shoes

Split skirts (culottes)

Sweaters tucked in

Denim jackets worn with dresses

Big polka dots

Big, scruffy purses

Bulky quilted bathrobes

Big, gimmicky hats

The "dowdy" look

The "harsh" look

White shoes before Easter or after Labor Day

Tattoos

Patterns that don't match

*Anything gaudy or overdone that calls more atten-
tion to the clothes than to the woman in them.*

SOMETHING IN THE WAY SHE MOVES

You can have all the right clothes, makeup, and accessories, but they'll go completely unnoticed unless you know how to move in them. Graceful, confident, and positive are three adjectives that should describe you in motion.

Your mother has probably been telling you for years to stand up straight, and it's about time you listen. Sit up straight as well, and never, horror of horrors, *never* sit with your legs wide apart, even when you're wearing pants and relaxing. Most rich will rapidly dismiss that as a gesture of ill-breeding.

Walk with your head up, your shoulders square, your back erect and always look as if you're headed toward some delicious liaison. It will make people want to know where you're going, and possibly want to come with you.

You may find this hard to believe, but my posture, and the aura I exude as I walk were responsible for starting a most scintillating and profitable relationship with a man I'll call Patrick.

Patrick was "Mr. Morning," one of the most popular and best-paid radio personalities in the city. I had to pass by his studio window every day as I walked to work. I returned his smiles and waves without thinking much about it, until he started taping signs for me on his window. On sheets of computer paper he would write single words like "classy," "beautiful," and "HOT!" with colored markers.

After about three weeks of this, on the day he hung the word "elegant," I decided to call the radio station and thank him. After all, he *was* going to a lot of effort, and the signs were actually quite amusing.

"This is 'Elegant,'" I told him when I finally got through. "I just want to tell you I appreciate the signs."

"Oh wow! Elegant!" he gushed. "I never thought I'd actually talk to you! Do you know you have an amazing walk? I look for it every morning. I even talk about it on the air! What's you real name? Where are you headed every day? Do you want to have lunch sometime?"

It took him several more weeks to get the requested information out of me. I don't give my full name or place of employment to anyone until I've done some serious investigation on them, and I especially didn't give it to radio people, who I'd heard could be rather slimy. I finally decided this one would be safe, however, and consented to a few lunches, which led to a few dinners, which led to many great experiences and beautiful gifts.

Some time later I asked, "What was it that prompted you to single me out of the hundreds of other women who pass by your window every day?"

"It was the way you carried yourself—your attitude, something in the way you move," he began crooning. "It said, 'I'm here, I'm hot, and I'm setting this beautiful world on fire.' I was like a moth to the flame."

Later I sat in his studio with him one morning, and began to understand what he was talking about. We watched what he called "the parade." Hundreds of women did pass by, many of them in beautiful clothes, but wearing expressions that said, "I hate mornings, and I hate the world." The money they spent on their expensive outfits was wasted by their scowls. A number of these women were busily puffing away on their last cigarette before they got to their office. They looked harsh and crude. The worst was a woman who wore a dress so tight it was obvious the temperature that morning was very low.

"She knows I'm here watching behind this one-way glass window," he told me. "Sometimes, when she thinks no one else is around, she'll open her blouse and flash her chest, or flip up her skirt and display other parts of her lingerie-free body. She thinks it's provocative. She has no idea how disgusting she is."

That morning was quite an education for me. I realized what a difference a smile and confident walk could make. I resolved to always remember this.$

THREE

Feeling Like A Million
From the Inside Out

Now that we've got those superficial things on the outside taken care of, it's time to turn our attention inside. You can look like a million bucks, but your soul should be priceless. Millionaires and many others know all too well that the outside is not necessarily a reflection of the inside, and if the men have any depth at all, they won't be fooled.

I have trouble mourning for my friend Sheila. She's one of the most beautiful women I know, and she spends thousands of hours and dollars to get that way. She's also able to get a date with anyone she pleases. But that's *a* date; singular. They never come back for more. "I don't know why they never call again," she laments. "You'd think I was a airhead or sumpthin'. I am not a airhead!" Sheila is not a bad person. She's just a little naive and shallow. If she spent half the time reading that she does doing her hair, she might develop a reason for a return visit. But as it is, Sheila bores most men to tears. They've told me so.

If Sheila were to ask, this is what I'd do for her to make her a more interesting and well-rounded woman, to make good company out of her, and to make her more compatible with the millionaires she so longs to ensnare.

A Crash Course in Culture

First I would expose my friend Sheila to all the arts. I would make her sit on my couch and go through my "art collection." Wherever I am in the world, I make it a point to visit the local art museum. I buy postcard sized prints of the paintings that are important, and of the paintings that I love. I have quite a collection now, and I keep it in a brocade box on my coffee table. Someday, I hope my children will lovingly sort through them. For now, I would let Sheila look at each one slowly, explaining why they are beautiful, dramatic, daring, well-composed, depressing, dangerous, enlightening, ingenious.

This would help to give her a sense of aesthetics, and perhaps be more appreciative and cognizant of the beauty around her. It would also help her discern between things that are well-done visually, and things that are poorly done.

If you don't have a friend with time and a box of pictures, I'd suggest you spend a few evenings in your local library, looking up great art by the masters. Better yet, take an art appreciation class at the local university or community college. Not all millionaires have a sense of visual aesthetics or taste, but they will appreciate yours, and you will be surprised at how often art comes up at elite social gatherings.

As Sheila and I are studying paintings, I would be playing great music in the background. She would be listening to classical pieces by the most famous composers, as well as jazz, modern instrumentalists and vocalists, American musicals, and ethnic music. I would try to help her gain an appreciation for all of it. I would like her to be able to discern the individual's styles and quality.

I have an extensive and discriminating CD collection, augmented greatly by the recording executive I see. One of the first things men do when they enter my home on their initial visit is go directly to my CD collection to discover what kind of taste I have. They're usually impressed by the eclecticism and quality of my disks, and when they spot some of their favorites, it's not uncommon for them to vow, right then and there, to take me to that concert, whether it's performed locally or in a distant city.

Sheila's homework would be to listen to National Public Radio for as many hours a day as she could—she wouldn't have to give it her undivided attention, but it would help her with current events and culture as well as with music. Once again, the library, with its books, tapes, CDs, and records, could be of assistance to her.

It would be a good idea for both you and Sheila to learn to appreciate as many different types of great music as you can. There will be music playing almost everywhere you go, and if you can identify it and enjoy it, you will get more out of the experience. You can help your date's enjoyment also—or he can help you, if he knows you're interested. It will be fascinating for him to discuss with you the music he's passionate about. Plus, it's one more topic on the old conversation list.

READING UP

Next I'd give Sheila a list of books to read. It would be a very eclectic list, and it would include everything from Shakespeare (to get a feel for a lyric mastery of the English language) to Michael Crichton, for although his literary merit is questionable, *everyone* is talking about his books these days. I'd have her read the good books that I have been happiest that I've read—the ones whose stories, ideas, or quotes have come up in more conversations with wealthy men than I can count. There are a number of books that can make a difference in her life—books that are must-reads if she wants to improve herself, and wants to be considered culturally literate, enriched, enlightened, and conversant.

I've mentioned a few of them on the next page, and I've whittled the list down to the ten easiest books to get through. You and Sheila should read as many of them as you can, but don't worry if you can't get to them all immediately. With each book you read, you'll find your world expand. I would suggest getting the Cliff notes if they're available, or some other study aid for these books. They'll help you with the deeper meanings and literary value. Also, underline or copy any quotes or ideas you particularly like. You'll want to refer to them later in letters, conversations, or just for your own personal enjoyment.

- *The Power of Myth*, by Joseph Campbell. Start here. It will give you broad information about history, art, religion, and philosophy. In addition, his theories are quite popular topics of conversation these days.

- *Hamlet,* by William Shakespeare. Read as much Shakespeare as you can, but if you can only read one play, this is it. You're probably familiar with more lines from this work than any other. It can be fun searching for them.

- *Atlas Shrugged*, by Ayn Rand. Her ideas are not the most humanitarian, and anything but altruistic, but she's a fascinating author, and many of her philosophies coincide with those of the very wealthy. It might help you understand them. I once snagged a man's undying affection merely by uttering the simple, famous phrase, "Who is John Galt?" Read the book to find out what this means.

- *The Complete Works of Robert Frost.* His poetry contains eloquent lines that touch everyone's heart at some time or other.

They're also easy to memorize. You'll find yourself referring to them often.

- The Bible. Don't be afraid to skip over the more technical parts, and go for one of the older, rather than the more modern translations—the wording will be more recognizable when you hear it quoted elsewhere. Even if you don't believe in God, this is one of the most influential books in our culture and you should be familiar with it.

- "The Latest," by Michael Crichton. That's not an actual book title, but read his latest work, whatever it may be. He is one of the most wildly popular authors around, and you'll get through his work quickly. You'll be able to compare it with the movie or television shows in conversations people are bound to be having every night.

- *The Road Less Traveled*, by M. Scott Peck. It's not exactly pop psychology, but it's very popular, and has some invaluable ideas you'll want to use in the relationships you'll be developing.

- *Crime and Punishment*, by Fyodor Dostoyevsky. Some people consider Russian literature hard to take, others swear it's the most fascinating writing they've ever read. I promise you there will be rewards if you can make it through this one.

- *Les Miserables,* by Victor Hugo. The abridged version will do nicely. It gives you the same wonderful story without Hugo's convoluted asides. You'll get much more out of the play after having read this book, plus you'll have an emotional experience. I challenge you not to cry.

- *1984*, by George Orwell. Ever hear of the term, "Orwellian?" Wondered what is meant by the phrase, "Big brother is watching"? Find out what they mean. This is the quickest read of all.

It will probably take Sheila at least a year to read these books, become familiar with them and digest them. But I wouldn't advise Sheila or you to stop when the list is completed. Ideally a "reading habit" will be developed. When there's nothing to do, a book will call your attention before anything else. Schedules will be arranged so there will be plenty of time to read.

Now, if all this looks painfully intimidating, don't despair! I have a little secret for you that can make you appear devastatingly literate in less than a month. Run to your nearest bookstore and buy *The Great American Bathroom Book*, "Single-Sitting Summaries of All-Time Great Books." This little treasure contains page-long summaries of not only the classics, but business management books, modern literature, and books on emotional and physical health. There's also an invaluable section in it called, "Trivia to Learn By." If you can retain only a fraction of the information this book has to offer, you'll be considered one of the most well-read members of any circle.

In addition, you need to keep up on current events. Every one should read at least one news magazine a week and try to see a paper every day. This does not include tabloids like *The National Enquirer* or *The Star*. No self-respecting person would encourage those publications by paying money for them, or even stoop to having them in their home. Stick with magazines and periodicals that have a reputation for accurate reporting. A well-read person *never* runs out of conversation and never ceases to grow.

Most millionaires read voraciously to stay on top of things. Sheila needs to find out what the ones she's involved with read, and read that too. Is he into *The*

Wall Street Journal? Science fiction? World history? *Sports Illustrated*? (There's one for you—almost every man on the face of the earth is into the swimsuit issue. She should get a hold of it before he does and ask him how he thinks she'd look in that gold number on page 47—it would overwhelm him).

You, Sheila, anyone can get something out of almost everything read. *Almost* everything. Some books you shouldn't even waste your time with. Time is invaluable you know, so try to spend it reading classics or books of current significance. Pornography and cheap romance novels are out, of course, and there is a certain amount of pride that can be derived from the ability to say that you don't do Stephen King, Jacqueline Suzanne, or other authors like them.

All this reading is going to require major investments of time. Where will Sheila get that? First, I'd advise her to keep her television off most of the time, unless the men she's interested in are involved with television production. Then she should watch their programs avidly. Otherwise, I'd say she should cut back on the sitcoms, the talk shows, the soaps. Those can eat up the major portion of her spare moments if she's not careful. And it is really not all that impressive if, every time a man calls or drops by, the

TV is blaring.

Now if you and Sheila follow the preceding suggestions, you'll be much better prepared intellectually and culturally to associate with the wealthy. Not all millionaires will know everything you know once you get all this down, and some will know volumes more. But when it comes to culture, you will at least be able to hold your own. Let the learning process continue. You can never know too much.

Let's proceed along those learning lines, and move into an area that can be either your crowning glory or your devastating downfall.

So You Say

Many people believe that it's not what you say, but how you say it. I can't tell you how many times I've found that to be true, from the time I was very young.

I remember my first feeble attempt at being polite in Spanish. I was at the San Diego Zoo, when a woman I thought looked Hispanic opened a gift shop door for me. "Grassy Ass!" I said to her with a smile, horribly mispronouncing the Spanish word for "Thank you." A stormy look came over the woman's face, and she pushed the door closed on me. My sister, who was observing the whole thing, doubled over in laughter, and explained to me later that the woman was Asian Indian, and was probably deeply offended by my faux pas.

Your speech can make you or break you. A well-turned phrase can be every bit as captivating as a well-tuned torso. I have seen men completely entranced by women who have unique ways of expressing themselves.

Millionaires are often information sponges, and many have been educated at the world's finest schools, so they find a woman with an interesting vocabulary both comfortable and intriguing. Eloquence is a sure-fire way to earn their respect right from the beginning. By the same token, poor grammar and pronunciation can quickly gain you their disdain.

If the millionaire has not had a stellar education, you can be assured that he will be somewhat insecure about it, and he'll consider an eloquent woman both a great prize and a learning opportunity.

Try to liberally pepper your speech with polysyllabic words. It's much more interesting to proclaim, "I'm absolutely ecstatic!" then to say, "Gee, I sure do feel good."

Learn a new word a day. Go to the library, pick up some back issues of *Readers Digest*, and xerox some copies of "It Pays to Enrich Your Word Power," or just go through the dictionary. There's also a great vocabulary section in *The Great American Bathroom Book*.

Make sure you know the pronunciation as well as the definition, however. If you're not sure how to say it or what it means, don't use it. I'll never forget the embarrassed blush on the face of a friend when she was told the word "omnipotent" was not pronounced "ahm-knee-POE-tent." She had just used the word in a job interview.

Then there's one millionaire's favorite faux pas: As he was driving her up a mountain to a beautiful resort, his date placed her hand over her ear and squealed, "Oooh! My fallopian tube just popped!"

Have fun with words. I do, and I've included a list of some of my favorites. The word 'pulchritude' raises eyebrows every time I use it, because no one else ever does. Practice some of these, and try incorporating them in your working vocabulary. Sorry—some you'll have to look up:

abscond	adroit	ambiguous
ambivalent	appall	apex
arbiter	archaic	banal
cacophony	cognizant	culpable

demigod	didactic	discerning
eclectic	ecstatic	erudite
esoteric	euphoric	exacerbate
excessive	fiasco	genre
gesticulate	gratuitous	inadvertent
innocuous	insatiable	intrinsic
jingoistic	juggernaut	latent
macabre	Machiavellian	malleable
maniacal	megalomania	minuscule
misnomer	misogynist	monosyllabic
morass	mundane	nefarious
omnipotent	opulent	paragon
penchant	pervasive	plethora
pulchritude	quixotic	reiterate
repartee	repast	sans
sacrosanct	scintillating	sumptuous
sycophant	titillating	vacuous
xenophobic		

YOU CAN'T SAY THAT

There are some words that you should try to completely eliminate from your vocabulary. "Uh" and "ain't" are probably the first utterances you'll think of, and they should go as well. But I'm particularly talking about those nasty vulgarities, many of them with four letters. And the profanities, which involve cavalierly throwing around the name of deity—anyone's deity. Both vulgarity and profanity are extremely offensive, and you should avoid them at all costs.

Most millionaires will hesitate to take you out in public if they fear a particularly graceless and abrasive word will spew from your lips. It simply lacks class.

If you're using them too often in your daily speech now, you won't be able to bridle them in more formal settings, so start watching your words and cutting back immediately. An occasional "hell" or "damn" won't condemn you, but in most situations you should be able to find more creative and accurate ways of expressing yourself.

There are times when, in the heat of passion, a strong word might leap out. That can sometimes serve to intensify things, but it can also shock and throw cold water on the situation. You'll have to use your own judgment, knowing your man as intimately as you should by the time you get there.

A Quick Grammar Lesson

This may surprise you, but there are many well-educated men who will silently and subconsciously dock you points when you use poor grammar. You will be left to blunder on unaware, never again receiving a call from that particular man, and wondering why you two didn't "click." I remember one extremely wealthy man calling me the day after a much-anticipated line-up, and telling me, "There's no way I could ever take her out again. She's a 'we-wuzer'" Poor grammar is a completely unnecessary speech impediment, and it should never put you at a disadvantage.

You must be careful, though. If you become too sensitive to poor grammar, you'll find yourself tempted to correct your millionaire in public. This will upset him, as it would you. Even if he asks you to correct him, don't do it in front of other people. That's just not courteous.

There are a few common grammatical errors that sound like fingernails scraping across a chalkboard to those who know English well. Don't be found guilty of using them! Read the following list, and never make these mistakes again.

- *Irregardless*. There is no such word. "Regardless" is correct.
- *I could care less*. If you really don't care, you want to say, "I couldn't care less." "I could

care less" means it might be slightly important to you.

- *I feel badly.* "Badly" is an adverb, and in this instance implies that your ability to touch things is impaired. It should be, "I feel bad."

- *What are you inferring by that?* "Infer" means to deduce or assume. You probably mean "imply," which means to suggest or hint.

- *I felt nauseous.* That means you felt as if you were making people sick. What you want to say is "I felt nauseated." (This is one of my personal favorites. I caught it in a book written by a millionaire I know. He should have paid more for a better editor.)

- *So he goes…* There are so many incorrect phrases that replace the word "said." Among them are "I'm all…" and "She's like…" They sound *very* unrefined. Use a correct verb.

- *I'm so anxious to meet you!* You might be anxious, but you wouldn't want to admit it. "Eager" is what you really want to say. "Anxious" has the same root as "anxiety," and indicates tension.

- *So I thought to myself…* Cut out those last two words. Who else can hear your thoughts other than yourself? That is redundant.

- *Between you and I*… That may sound right, but it's not. It should be "between you and me." Use "me" after a preposition.

- *If I was you*… Make that "if I were you." When it's contrary to reality, use "were."

- *So I says*… When you stop to think about that, you know it's not right. But most people fire it off when they're speaking quickly. Listen for it. Its frequency will sicken you. It should be "So I said."

- *Where is it at?* That's another one that's obvious when you slow down. Always leave off the "at." Grammar is becoming less formal these days, and on occasion it's acceptable to end a sentence in a preposition, but never in this instance. Avoid "Where are we going to?" as well.

- And now for the endin'. *Always* say your complete 'ing's. Never stop at the 'n.'

PHRASES THAT NEVER PAY

There are some expressions that are tossed into conversations and land with an ugly thud. Then they seem to just sit there, exuding a vile stench. These are coarse expressions that can suck the life right out of an energetic dialogue.

They usually refer to the body, and while I hate
to even write them, I'll list some so you can be sure
to avoid them. Some I refuse to print, but you'll get
the general idea. It's strange that men will often say
them to their best friends, but as soon as a woman
uses them, they think she's trashy. Anyway, here are
some of them:

> *"I almost peed my pants."*
>
> *"I was up to my ass in…"*
>
> *"He could've s—t a brick."*
>
> *"We were really pissed off."*
>
> *"She had tits out to there."*
>
> *"Son of a b—h."*
>
> *"F—k that!"*

Avoid these and similar expressions like you'd
avoid a man in a polyester bowling shirt. They are
dead giveaways of a lack of refinement.

Now, last but not least when it comes to appropriate speech, there are two questions you should
never ask any adult. They are none of your business,
and show a lack of breeding. These two questions
are:

> *"How much did it cost?"* and *"How old are you?"*

If you can incorporate all these ideas into your

speech patterns, you will be doing wonderfully well. Now you only have a few more skills to acquire before you're ready to swim with those diamond bedecked sharks.

MIND YOUR MANNERS

Another skill to master is the fine art of etiquette. This also can be self-taught. Go to the library or purchase a book for your own personal edification, and pore over it. These books are actually great fun, and you will be amazed at how well the details will stick with you even if you're not trying actively to memorize them. Focus especially on meal manners and introductions, since you'll be in those two situations most frequently.

While it's not necessary for the rules of etiquette to cause you major stress, you should know that if anyone is going to notice a lack, it will be the wealthy. Many of them still send their children to some sort of charm school, and since they're in formal situations more often than the rest of us, they pay a little more attention to the rules of formality.

I wish I would have paid more attention to those rules before I attended a formal dinner with Craig. Craig's father was a superlatively important businessman with international interests, and one night we found him entertaining dignitaries from all over the world. Craig and I were invited to join the dinner party. This was the first time I had met Craig's father, and I watched him closely, fascinated by his ability to draw everyone at the table into the conversation.

Among some unidentifiable exotic delicacies, I was relieved to find angel hair pasta on my plate. I thought it would be infantile and insulting to chop the pasta into bite-sized pieces, (as I later learned the etiquette books suggest), and I decided to show how truly continental I could be by winding it around my fork, guided by my spoon, the way I'd seen Italians do it in Rome. It wasn't working. Tangled, drippy masses were squirming from my plate to my mouth and back again.

Just as I was losing a battle with a particularly nasty strand, Craig's father decided it was my turn to be included in the conversation. He turned his eyes on me, and all eyes at the table followed. They caught me just in time to see me quickly slurp up a long strand of pasta, which whipped up and hit me in the nose, splashing sauce all over my face, just before it disappeared into my mouth. I didn't make an exceptional impression on Craig's father. That was the last time I was invited to dinner at his house.

It all could have been avoided if I had paid more attention to practical etiquette. I'll now take you through a typical evening, applying some of the rules you'll use most often.

- If your date says he will pick you up at 7:00 P.M., be ready at 7:00 P.M. Making him wait 20 minutes while you finish your makeup is not cute or coy, it's inexcusable.

- If your date is going to be more than ten minutes late, he should phone you. If you have not heard from him and he is more than 45 minutes late, consider the date off and leave. You have your own life, and he has no right to expect you to wait around.

- When he comes to your door, invite him in for a moment while you collect your purse, coat, whatever. Two or three minutes of last minute primping is acceptable. You should already have seen to it that your home is clean and comfortable. Invite him to sit down, and make sure that no pets, children, or parents are annoying him. If you are old enough to go out with a millionaire, your parents should realize that it would be offensive to give him the third degree.

- When you are ready to go, if it is a cold night, extend your coat to him and let him help you put it on. Let him open and close doors for you, and walk on the side nearest the street when you are on foot. Take his arm or his hand, if it is offered. This is not so much a sign of possession as a sign of courtesy. These customs may seem old-fashioned, but many wealthy men pride themselves in being gallant, and will be disappointed if you do not allow them these common courtesies.

- When entering a car or limousine, allow the door to be opened for you, sit down on the seat, then swing both legs in together. When disembarking, permit your date or his chauffeur to open the door, and gracefully swing both legs out at the same time. Take the man's hand, if it is offered, place your weight evenly on both feet, and stand up.

These methods are not always possible, however, especially if the vehicle is much higher or lower than the standard size. In that case, enter the vehicle as gracefully as you can while keeping your knees together. In the car, sit as close to your date as the seatbelt will allow. Safety first.

- When you are introduced to someone, as the woman you may offer your hand if you wish. It is not essential. You should, however, look them in the eye, smile, repeat their name, and say how nice it is to meet them. Something like, "Mr. Harwood, how good it is to meet you." Say it sincerely, not as if it's the automatic response to every introduction. You might want to add something positive to that, like "I've heard so many wonderful things about you."

- Try as hard as you can to remember all names given. But one day you will inevitably come across a situation where you've forgotten a name and are obligated to make introductions. The best you can do is to "forget" to mention the name, and say, "I'd like you to meet Michael Hironaka." Then Michael can say, "Hello, I'm sorry—I didn't catch your name." You should be ready to do the same for Michael if the need arises. If someone has forgotten your name, never say anything embarrassing like "You don't remember me, do you?" Politely remind them of your name and where you met: "Amanda Whittaker—we met at Collette Jackson's wedding reception."

- When you are the one making the introductions, there is a specific order to follow. The full name of the older person, the woman, or the most prominent person should always be spoken first, followed by, "I'd like you to meet…" Always give the first and last name. Do not worry about qualifying your relationships in the introduction. Avoid phrases such as, "This is my friend Michael." Michael would be offended if he considers himself more than a friend, and so would you. Just say, "Senator Hamlisch, this is Michael Hironaka."

If a conversation is to follow the introduction, I like to make presentations with a mention of something the two have in common, such as, "Senator Hamlisch, this is Michael Hironaka. He's almost as impressive on the back nine at Ravenscrest as you are." That way they can immediately begin conversing about golf. If your date is making the introductions, hopefully he will afford you the same courtesy.

- If you are in a restaurant, you walk directly behind the headwaiter to your table. Your date will follow. Allow the headwaiter to pull out your chair. Sit down, then rise slightly, allowing either the headwaiter or your date to push the chair farther up to the table. Try to do this as gracefully as possible.

- Once you are seated, place your napkin on your lap immediately, unless you are attending a dinner party, in which case you wait for your hostess to place her napkin. Never tuck it into your collar or belt. (Men have more of a problem with this than women.)

- Your date should ask you about your order, then give it to the waiter. When the waiter asks a direct question of you, such as "What kind of salad dressing would you like? Answer him directly, rather than going through your date. No matter how wealthy your escort is, it is bad form to order the most expensive item on the menu. It is equally bad form to order the least expensive item. If you are confused, ask your date what he would suggest. Don't make a habit of ordering exactly the same thing he does, however. It might give him the impression that you cannot make decisions on your own.

- If you are confused by an overabundance of serving utensils at your place setting, (and you could easily come across three knives, three forks, three spoons, and four glasses, plus numerous other plates and dishes), take your cue from your host—wait until he picks one up, to see which one to use. When this fails, use the "outside in" rule. You use the utensil farthest from your plate first, and work in.

- While eating, avoid making unnecessary noises with your food, chair, dishes or silverware. *Never* chew gum, or take it out of your mouth and set it on the side of your plate. You shouldn't have been chewing gum in the first place. The most delicate way to dispose of it is to swallow it. Sound disgusting? Then to avoid this situation, refrain from chewing gum—ever.

- The American-style of eating, where you cut your food with your knife in your right hand, then put it down and use your fork in your right hand when you are ready to take a bite, is acceptable. The European-style is acceptable too, however. That's when you cut with the knife in the right hand, and eat with the fork, tines down, in the left hand.

- Do not take a drink if there is already food in your mouth. Do not take huge mouthfuls of anything, and do not take a half-bite of food from your spoon or fork. Don't cut up your whole meal before you eat it—cut only one or two bites at a time.

Break off a small piece at a time from your bread and butter it—never butter the whole thing at once, unless it is hot and better with melted butter. It is correct to cut your salad with a knife if the pieces are too big to gracefully put in your mouth.

- If you come across a mouthful of something that is spoiled or has a bone, rock, or any other foreign matter in it, quietly remove it from your mouth with your fork or your fingers, then set it discreetly on the side of your plate. Do not say anything about it if it would offend your host or hostess.

- If you are dining at someone's home and spill something on the table, try to remove it with the edge of your knife, and put the spilled matter on the edge of your plate. If it has left a stain, use a little water from your water glass on your napkin to try to dab it away. Discreetly apologize to your hostess. If you spill liquid in a restaurant, quickly catch the waiter, who should bring a napkin to cover the spot. If you are at someone's home, immediately ask the hostess where you can find a sponge or cloth, and clean it up.

- Do not touch your hair when you are at the table. It is, however, permissible to delicately re-do your lipstick when you are finished. If you have to cough, sneeze, or blow your nose, it is not necessary to leave the table, but you should cover your nose and mouth with a handkerchief. Never blow your nose into your napkin.

- When you are finished with your meal, do not push your plate back or announce, "I'm full!" or "That's enough for me!" and especially not, "I'm stuffed!" (the former is in particularly bad taste among the British, to whom that expression has a very negative connotation.) Place your napkin at the side of your plate, neither folded nor crumpled, and place your utensils together, diagonally across your plate. That is signal enough that you are through.

- If you are attending a dinner party, it is appropriate to stay at least one hour after dinner, otherwise it seems as if you are "eating and running." When leaving a party, *always* find the host and/or hostess, wait until they are done conversing with whomever, then thank them graciously.

- Within a week of the event, especially if it included an overnight stay, send a brief thank-you note to those who hosted. It should express your gratitude for the invitation and your enjoyment of the event. While this is not a requirement, it is always appreciated. Even if your date was the host and it was just the two of you, he will enjoy receiving a note of appreciation.

BE A SPORT

A very important thing to remember about millionaires is that almost all of them are recreationally active. Some have more leisure time than the rest of us and they fill it up with participatory sports. Others are working so hard that their leisure time is very precious to them, and they fill it up with exhilarating and elite physical activities.

Also, some sports are considered socially de rigueur if you travel in the greater economic circles. If you want to get a piece of a wealthy man's leisure time, you'll need to be able to keep up with him. The more sports you can manage to learn, the better chance you'll have of accompanying them when they play. Certain skills are a must. They are:

SWIMMING

Better yet, scuba diving. Take advantage of community courses in your area, which are generally inexpensive, to learn and become adroit at these sports skills. So much wealthy social activity takes place around pools, beaches, and boats. You wouldn't want to pass any of that up because of your fear of the water. You also wouldn't want to pass on a trip to the Bahamas because you are not scuba certified. Learning to water-ski, sail, and kayak is useful too, but not absolutely essential.

GOLF

I could have kicked myself for not keeping my golf skills up. I took lessons when I was younger, but hadn't touched a club in years when the millionaire I was dating at the time asked me to complete a foursome. It seemed he was entertaining a couple of Japanese businessmen, and they were going to take a helicopter over the autumn-colored landscape to a remote golf course buried in a mountain valley. I had to pass because my golf skills were nonexistent at that point, but I signed up for a community education refresher course as soon as possible.

If you're even remotely skilled, you'll be called on to play golf with your wealthy man's business associates and/or their spouses quite frequently. A lot of business is conducted on the golf course, and you don't want to be left out. Also, if you know what you're doing, the golf course is a great place to meet the economically gifted. More on that later.

Even if you play poorly, show some enthusiasm and a basic knowledge of the sport. Recently I confessed to a wealthy man I was seeing that I was not exactly adept on the links. Because he wanted me to enjoy the sport with him, he immediately signed me up for a series of private lessons with a pro, and then bought me my own equipment—top of the line clubs, bag, shoes, balls, etc.

SNOW SKI

My first experience with snow-skiing left me on crutches for several months with torn ligaments. I resisted my friends' efforts to get me back on the slopes for years, until I started dating the son of the owner of a ski resort. Everything was fine through the summer when we did a lot of hiking and ballooning (sports which require little skill but a fair amount of stamina), but as winter set in, I realized that skiing was his life, and if I wanted to be part of it, I'd better conquer the slopes.

I secretly went out and bought decent equipment, deciding that if I invested some money in the sport, I'd have more incentive to learn. I then enrolled in a promotional ski school offered by the a newspaper and a local resort—four classes for ten bucks—it couldn't be beat. In a few short weeks I was ready to ski with him, or so I thought. Next to his, my skiing was pathetic, and I wished that I would have succumbed to my friends' pleadings to get me on the slopes years earlier.

At this point I'm still only a fair skier, but I couldn't be happier that I took up the sport. It's tremendously satisfying, invigorating, and just plain fun. Plus it would be a shame to have to pass up the invitations to spend weekends in luxurious mountain condos with wealthy friends, just because I didn't know how to ski. Learn. It will open up whole new worlds for you.

TENNIS

Tennis is a very social sport. Wealthy men often play tennis with each other, and as with golf, you'll often be called on to play doubles with the wealthy men's friends, spouses, or companions. Their country clubs will have tournaments as well, and your millionaire friend will be thrilled if you two can make a few rounds as a doubles team. In addition, it's just a fun, active date to go to his club for a few sets and lunch. Make sure you have the proper white attire, though. Some clubs are very picky about that, and your millionaire will probably forget to tell you, assuming you already know. Ask at the local tennis shop, or call the club in advance to find out.

There are other sports that it wouldn't hurt you to know—horseback riding, racquetball, shooting (hunting), sky-diving, motorcycle riding, squash, fishing, cross-country skiing, the list is endless. But you certainly don't have to master all of them, and not all at once. Attack the ones mentioned in detail first, then move on to the others if time and finances allow.

It is essential, however, that you also have a working knowledge of spectator sports. Basketball, baseball, and football are musts, since there is a good chance your millionaire will have season tickets to at least one professional team's season. Your millionaire might even be involved in playing one of them, and in that case it is imperative that you appreciate and understand what he is doing. Your knowledge will help you catch him in the first place.

Also, be familiar with horse racing, auto racing, and polo. You'll find the wealthy at all these events, and will probably be invited to accompany your friend to some of them. It's nice if you can appear marginally knowledgeable and conversant about them, and don't have to pester your millionaire with silly questions.

Acquiring these skills and knowledge might seem like a tall, impossible order, but let me assure you, you can do it in a surprisingly short time. Besides, working on them will get you out and active, will stretch your body and your mind, and will allow you to make some new and interesting friends. You won't regret the time you spend in these pursuits, I promise.

A Basic Course in Relationship Ethics

We've worked on your cultural awareness, on your intellect, on your physical skills and on your speech. Now it's time to tidy up your very core—your integrity. Some people will find this advice terribly moralistic, others will find it blatantly obvious. But when it comes to relationships, it should be considered good, common sense. These admonitions are essential for living and growing in harmony with another human being, for developing a quality relationship that lasts. I shouldn't even have to mention them, but things have a strange way of getting twisted these days and people get confused. If you're not living them, commit to them now and start immediately.

- *Never date a married man.* Don't even think about it. First of all, you're a fool to believe he will leave his wife, no matter what he says, and second, how could you think of devastating his spouse, a woman you probably don't even know? I can guarantee you she's not the shrew he says she is. Third, if he cheats on his wife, he'll cheat on you. Be assured of that.

- *Never go out on your husband.* You should be ashamed of yourself for even reading this book if you're married. How could you stand yourself, knowing that you've broken one of the most important promises you'll ever make? It shows that you have a very serious character flaw. I don't care if "everyone" does it. That's society's problem, not yours. If you're unhappy in your marriage, get out of it before you even think of straying. Save your self-respect and your husband's feelings.

- *Don't do recreational drugs.* No one is going to appreciate the prospect of your snorting away time, money, and life. A drug addiction shows that you have problems with self-control and good judgment. Drugs (including alcohol) are damaging. If you wouldn't want your kids to do them, you shouldn't do them either.

- *Always practice safe sex.* We all know that the safest sex is abstinence. But when that just isn't going to occur, until you're married, insist that he wear a condom, no matter what he says about his sexual history. He's almost always hiding something, or might be very sincere and just not know. Unless he can show you a medical statement signed within the last few days, *make him wear a condom.*

- *Never be involved in a fatal attraction situation.* Let him go gracefully, and don't consider damaging his property or other relationships. Sever him from your life and move on.

- *Never ask for or accept money from your "significant other."* This can easily be misinterpreted as a sign that you can be bought, like any other possession. I personally never ask for anything, and I have a hard time accepting some gifts. When I do, however, I make sure the giver knows that there are no strings attached. If he thinks differently, I'm ready to give the gift back at any time.

- *Always be honest.* Never lie. It's sure to catch up with you, and it just gets too complicated. If there's a situation you think you need to lie about, clear it up, or make sure it never happens. Don't do anything that would give you a reason to be deceitful.

- *Never make yourself look good at another's expense.* This is cheap and petty. Let your merits stand on their own. You don't have to compare yourself with others. There's plenty of room for everyone to shine. Tarnishing someone else's reputation is completely unnecessary and completely classless.

- *Follow the golden rule.* "Do unto others as you would have others do unto you." Now *those* are words to live by.

AN ATTITUDE ADJUSTMENT

When I say the word 'men,' what images pop into your mind? Do you think of slimy scumballs out to take advantage of poor, long-suffering women, or do you think of a provocative species, somewhat different from your own, but intriguing and enjoyable none the less? Your attitude will scream loud and clear through your facade, so you'd better examine that attitude, and adjust it when necessary.

All our attitudes need adjusting at times, depending on the experiences immediately preceding them. My own attitudes are not immune to nosedives on occasion, and thank heavens I have good friends who can help straighten me out.

I was at a particularly low point when I had dinner with Jerome. Jerome owns a cadre of car dealerships, and is just a friend, but in that department he's unsurpassed. It seems I'd been extremely disappointed by the wealthy rogue I'd been dating, I'd found out my father was having an affair, and one of my dearest friend's husbands had just left her. My attitude about men was not at its shining best when Jerome came to pick me up.

"L.A.," he asked subtly, "what is your goal at the present time?"

"What I'd really like to do is develop a comfortable, romantic relationship with someone I can trust," I said.

"Why haven't you reached that goal? There are plenty of men out there."

"Because men are pigs!" I exploded. "They all have such glaring fatal flaws. Every single one of them is subversive, stupid, egotistical, selfish, and they have three-minute attention spans! Present company excluded, of course, Jerome."

"That's some attitude," he responded. "Let's look at this for a minute. Let's say I have a car salesman working for me and his goal is to simply sell a car, but he hasn't sold any. I ask him why—there are plenty of customers out there. He says, 'It's because customers are pigs! They all have such glaring fatal flaws. Every single one of them is subversive, stupid, egotistical, selfish, and they have three-minute attention spans!' Do you think the problem is with the customers or with the salesman? And do you think it would be easier for him to change the customers, or to change himself?"

I began to smile. I knew exactly what Jerome was talking about, and I realized I'd have to do some adjusting.

Because of the vast number of women after them, millionaires are usually able to discern rather quickly how you feel about them and how you feel about men in general. Even if she's put on her best party face, a woman's bitterness will show through and ward off rich men. Most wealthy men will not feel it's their duty to save you from your attitude, or try to be 'The One' who can prove to you that men are indeed noble. Instead they will continue their search for more pleasing company.

Even if your father was a rat, your high school sweetheart was a dog, and your ex-husband was a louse, it does not mean that all men are like that. Look around you. There must be some men in your circle who are respectable. And look beyond that. Aren't there any admirable community leaders in the vicinity? Neighbors, relatives, religious leaders, mailmen? I personally don't believe men are any better or any worse than women, it's just that many of us are more vulnerable to members of the opposite sex, and we can be deeply wounded by them. It doesn't mean they're out to get us, however. There are a good number who are out to help us.

If your attitude about men needs adjustment, focus on those good men around you. Realize that we're all human, and as humans we all have our strengths and our weaknesses. Try to concentrate on the strengths for a while to build your respect.

A very basic truth is that men like women who like men. It might seem difficult at first, but try to truly *like* men—and women too, for that matter. It's an art, and one well worth developing.

YOU'VE GOT TO HAVE FRIENDS

Probably one of the most essential skills you'll need to develop while working from the inside out is the art of making and keeping great friends. Don't think friends are imperative only so they can introduce you to their wealthy acquaintances. Friends are necessary for your own personal well-being and for happy human survival.

Take note of this conversation I had with Celeste, a beautiful, exotic, very out-going woman I roomed with in college. She's accustomed to having a number of monetarily endowed suitors on the line at any given moment, but a few months ago her supply had withered away to nothing. We all go through dry spells. This is how she handled it:

"You know I'm disappointed, but I really can't be too down about it. My life is so good, and I have such wonderful long-term friends, a little harsh luck in the romance department is just not enough to depress me."

She then thanked me for being her friend and for listening to her tales of woe, and then she told me she loved me. That made *me* feel wonderful. Even when Celeste was not in the greatest of humors, she went out of her way to do something nice for me. And you know, it made her feel much better as well.

Contrast Celeste's attitude with Dawn's. Dawn had hit some hard times, and complained that she was suicidal. She constantly whined to the few people who would listen that her only friends were her ex-husband and her therapist. Unfortunately, they felt more of a responsibility for her than a friendship. She became very demanding of their time, and eventually alienated them. "You've got to go out and make some real friends of your own," they admonished her before hanging up or closing the door. Her self-absorption had left her very lonely.

If you don't know how to establish good, healthy, platonic relationships, who will be there to support you when your millionaire du jour leaves you reeling? Who will help you see things from an objective point of view when you're feeling rash? Who will keep you from becoming suffocatingly clingy to and dependent on your man? Who will give you outside input and ideas to make you more interesting? Who will you be able to practice relationship skills with? Who will keep you from becoming self-, or relationship, obsessed?

Friendships are essential to your well-being. In assessing the state of your friendships—with members of either sex, you might ask yourself the following questions:

- Do I have at least one friend who would come and pick me up at the airport at any hour of the day or night?

- Is there at least one friend in my life whom I would pick up at the airport at any hour of the day or night?

- Is there a platonic person in my life who I can talk to on the phone for two hours, then look down at my watch and be surprised that it's been more than ten minutes?

- Do I have a friend with whom I could easily get together three nights in a row, and not grow tired of her, or have her grow tired of me?

- Do I have a friend who, when she's sick, I'd drop everything to bring her the food or medicine she needed? Is there a friend out there who would do the same for me?

- Is there a friend in my life whom I can call long-distance and not worry about the expense, because I feel communication with that person is more important? Is there someone who would call me with those same feelings?

- Do I have a friend who would actually offer to help me move, without being asked? Would I offer to help someone under those same circumstances?

- Is there someone, other than a family member, who would trust me with her car? Would I trust her with mine?

- Do I feel good without my makeup on around any of my friends?

- Do I have a friend to whom I can say, "I love you?"

- Is there someone I can trust to be honest with me when I'm having a bad hair day, and who will help me fix it?

- Do I have a friend whom I could trust with the key to my house, room, or apartment? Is there someone who could trust me with theirs?

- Is there a friend around who would line me up with her rich, gorgeous brother?

The best romantic relationships evolve between two people who can also establish a good friendship. You'll know your relationship with a millionaire is really going somewhere if he is the answer to all the above questions. Of course there will be others in your life who can qualify as well—your millionaire should never become your only close friend.

Friendship, like love, does not just jump into your lap and stay there. You need to stroke it, cuddle it, make it purr. And you'll need to get in quite a bit of practice, because you'll make a few mistakes the first time around. It may dig its claws into you on its way out, but with experience, you'll learn how to deal with the pain. Pain is not necessarily bad. It helps you grow.

Friendship can be a great dry-run for romance, and it can also be an invaluable support before, during, and after. Learn how to cultivate it, nurture it, strengthen it, cherish it. It will make you a much more stable person, and a much more desirable friend.

Here are a few rules for friendship that can also apply to your association with your romantic interest. Most rules for good relationships work for both. You should never:

Borrow money from friends

Betray confidences

Constantly complain and whine

Be burdensome, tiresome, or taxing

Be afraid or slow to apologize

Get jealous

Become possessive

Interrupt

Moralize

Always share your worst with them because you are

so comfortable around them
Lecture
Stand them up
Arrive or call late, unless it's an emergency
Cancel at the last minute
Be hesitant to tell them you care

Incidentally, some of my dearest friends are millionaire ex-boyfriends. Our romance might not have endured, but we like each other so much as friends we just can't give up on the relationship. When they ask me for advice about a woman they're dating, and they always do, I tell them to look at her life and see how she treats her friends. Does she have many? Does she get along well with other females? Does she seem to truly treasure those platonic relationships? If the answer is 'yes' to those questions, I'll usually encourage him to go forward with her. You can tell a lot about people's true qualities by the way they treat their friends. **$**

FOUR

Identifying the Species:
What Is It You Want?

Now that you are everything a millionaire could possibly desire, you'll have to ask yourself this question: What do I want in a millionaire? It should take far more than mere money to entertain you and to possibly win your heart. To better identify your target, ask yourself the following questions:

How much older than I can he be?
How much younger?
Is it important how he made his money?

Is it important that he have an education?

How many character flaws am I willing to put up with for the benefit of his money?

How rich do I want him to be?

Does it matter to me whether his money is earned or inherited?

What kinds of physical standards do I require of him? Must he have hair? Can he be shorter than I? Etc.

What are my goals in dating him? Do I want to get married, or just have a good time?

Does a common religion matter to me?

Does a common ethnic background matter to me?

Does a common cultural background matter to me?

Do previous marriages make a difference?

Does he have a difficult ex-wife?

Does he have children, and how are they involved in his life?

Does he want to have more children, and if not, does it matter to me?

Are similar goals important to me?

Are similar interests important to me, and if so, how many?

Would I be willing to get involved in a long-distance relationship with him?

Use the answers to these questions to get a clear

picture of the ideal man you're looking for, but don't rule one out just because he doesn't meet all your criteria. If you wanted a man with old money and you come across a man who made his own fortune, for heaven's sake try to adjust! They can both provide you with the same kinds of experiences! You might consider expanding your horizons in a number of areas.

I was talking to Jill just the other day, who told me she had been very happy in a relationship until she discovered a fatal flaw: her boyfriend was ten years older than she was! I had to laugh at her gasps as I told her that some of my most rewarding relationships have been with men old enough to be my father. She was horrified.

I explained to her that older men are not threatened by the meager success I've accomplished, but instead, they encourage me. They also bring into a relationship wisdom, savvy, and experience that I find fascinating. And, on a more mercenary level, they're usually more generous in providing luxurious experiences and gifts, since most have made their fortunes by the time they reach their fifties. Then there's the fact that younger women are often a status symbol to older men, and they treat you as if you were a great prize.

While she's at it, Jill also might consider a man several years younger. All younger men are not looking for lithesome lingerie models. Shamelessly rich Gordon lost his mother when he was very young, and ended up marrying a woman 15 years his senior. He and his wife are one of the happiest couples I know. She is amused and entertained by his stamina, and she appreciates the fact that he is not emotionally scarred by years of serious relationships gone sour. He appreciates her for her wisdom, her ability to love, which has increased with her years, and for the security she brings him. Age is no more than what you make of it.

You might want to consider broadening your physical standards as well. I have another friend, Cynthia, who was obsessed with physical appearance, hair in particular. She required great masses of it on her men's heads, but not on their backs or shoulders. Picky, picky, picky. She said she wouldn't even consider a man with a shiny pate—until she saw my pictures of a recent vacation in Mexico. There I stood, wrapped in the arms of a very buff but very bald man, his beachfront mansion gleaming in the background. "His favorite expression is, 'Why waste perfectly good hormones growing hair?'" I told her. Cynthia has since changed her tune.

Consider opening your mind a bit. Don't think of it as sacrificing your standards, try to see it as broadening your horizons. Your chances of dating a millionaire will multiply as your ability be flexible expands.

I suppose my ideal millionaire would have been wealthy for some time and acquired refined tastes. He would be subtle about his wealth, but he would be passionate about the causes he believed in, including me. He would not have been married before (he's waited all those years for me, of course). He would be generous but not foolish, be kind, have a good sense of humor, and be able to associate with people from all walks of life. Most important, integrity would be his middle name. Hmmm…he sounds a little too good to be true. He probably is, since in all my experience I haven't met him yet. But as I have searched for him, I've met some delightful people who have greatly enriched my life. I'm positive my ideal can be adjusted under the right circumstances. I'm particularly susceptible to any man who can enrich my life in any way—not just monetarily.

You want someone who can enrich your life as well. But in your efforts to be open-minded about this, beware. There are a few types you will want to avoid. Be on the lookout for them, and steer clear.

THE PRETENDERS

First you need to know some basic danger signals.

The most important one of all states that if he talks too much about being a millionaire, he probably isn't one. He's a bona fide wannabe. Never believe the man who is crass enough to tell you all about his wealth in the first meeting. He's trying too hard to impress and convince you. Some women are incredibly naive, and will believe whatever a man tells them. Take Maria, for example.

"I'm getting married to a millionaire," she told us one day, after returning from a stay in California.

"That's great," we replied. "How long have you known your lucky fiancé?"

"Oh, about three weeks."

"And how did you meet him?"

"Well, he lives in the same apartment complex in Van Nuys as some girlfriends of mine. We met out by the pool."

"Really? What's a millionaire doing in an apartment complex like that?"

"Oh, it's only temporary. As soon as we're married, he's going to build a virtual palace for us!"

"That sounds great. What does he do for a living?"

"He's a famous author."

"Hmmm…What has he written? Do you think he's any good?"

"Well, I haven't seen any of his work, but he must be fantastic to make all that money from it. Of course, that's just a sideline. He has several car dealerships as well."

"So what kinds of dealerships does he own?"

"I'm not sure. His chiropractic practice keeps him so busy he hardly has time to check on the dealerships."

This woman was dead serious. She wasn't trying to impress us. She'd soaked in everything he told her. I think she and her fiancé both ought to be locked up, in separate kinds of institutions, of course.

Then there's Sharon, who actually has a master's degree. I'm at her place one night, admiring the home she's just purchased. At about 11:30 p.m. a man appears at her door. He's clutching a cheap wine bottle with about an inch of liquid sloshing around in the bottom. To my surprise, she actually invites him in.

"Who's *that*?" I inquire as I follow her to the kitchen to fetch a wine glass for her visitor's remains.

"Don't let his appearance or his manners fool you," she tells me in a whisper. That man is a television genius. He's got three Emmy's to his name."

"Right!" I reply. "What's he doing here, miles from either coast, where most major TV production takes place?"

"Well, he says he got sick of the rat-race," she answers earnestly. "He wanted to take some time off to kick-back and relax, so he's selling appliances down at Silo. That's were I met him."

I make allowances for Sharon because she is recently divorced, but I hope she wises up soon before anyone does serious damage to her.

Beware the man who talks too much about his wealth or achievements. Also beware the man who flashes them. If he drives a ridiculously expensive car, wears lots of jewelry, and makes a big show of spreading large sums around, he either:

A. Came about that money illegally.
B. Is using someone else's money.
C. Just recently acquired it, and won't have it for long.

My former roommate Sandy found that out the hard way. She couldn't believe her luck when Darrin, the richest man in town, came zooming up to her door in his outrageous luxury car. He toted the biggest diamond she'd ever seen, and offered to buy her a huge, designer home on the hill. He'd made his money in real estate, he told her. How could she resist? Before long she was a happily married woman, and all her friends and family were investing in her husband's no-risk real estate projects.

Not long ago Darrin was released from prison. Sandy helped put him there. Darrin was swindling everyone he came close to. Sandy had the marriage annulled.

It's usually quite easy to spot a flamboyant fraud. The ones that can do serious damage are the ones who are crafty about it.

"I can always spot a rich man by the elegant way he dresses," says Delonna. "I look at the way his clothes are tailored, the fabric they're made of. I pay attention to small details like his ties, his watch, and especially his shoes."

Delonna can easily be deceived. The quickest and easiest way in the world to change your image is to change your clothes. For a thousand dollars or less, a man can easily take on the appearance of a millionaire. There are so many designer knock-offs these days, it's hard to tell the fake from the authentic. For about $30, you can pick up a faux Rolex on the streets of New York City that can fool experts at first glance.

Bigger items can be counterfeited as well. A fine automobile can be rented or borrowed, as can a large house, boat or plane. They can also put a man in tremendous debt, so he barely has the money to scrape by

BECOME A PRIVATE INVESTIGATOR

So how then do you differentiate the authentics from the impostors?

One way is to do your homework on the man. If he says he's involved in certain fields, press him for details. Get the names of specific corporations he's involved with, and ask him his position. Then call that corporation to verify it. Don't reveal who you are, simply say, "I'd like to speak to your chief executive officer, Mr. Charles Chamberlain." If they say they've never heard of such a person, you know your "prince" is probably a pauper. If they connect you promptly, hang up before he comes on the line.

A business card will greatly aid you in your research. If he doesn't offer you one, it is not inappropriate to request one. Think up a good excuse to ask for his card, such as "that's a very interesting field to be in. I'd like to get more information on it. Is there an address I could write to request some?"

If his business card promotes his own company, look it up. Call the number. Drive past the address. Many times unstable or start-up businesses will list a "suite number" that is really a post-office box, or their own apartment. You'll want to check this out. Don't trust a man who leads you to believe he's more successful than he is.

If the research you do on the man doesn't tell you enough and he is persistent in his pursuit, agree to lunch with him. Lunch is a harmless, public situation, and your time is almost always limited, which is important. Note where he takes you and how he is treated there.

Cameron was trying to impress me, so he invited me to lunch at the city's oldest and most exclusive club. "I eat there all the time," he bragged. When we walked in, he was greeted coldly by the host and asked his name. Cameron said he was a guest of Donald Salton, a long-time member.

"Where would you like to dine?" the host inquired.

"In the club room, of course," Cameron replied.

"I'm sorry, but that is reserved for members only."

"How about the main dining room?" Cameron asked.

"That would be fine, sir, but I'm afraid that you

are not wearing a jacket, and one cannot dine in the main dining room without a jacket. Would you like to borrow one of ours?"

"No way," Cameron replied. "I don't want to wear someone else's jacket that wouldn't fit and probably smells. C'mon, L.A.—let's just go across the street."

Across the street we had fish and chips. "I tried," he said, lips glistening greasily. But for some reason, I didn't get the impression he'd tried very hard. Someone who was acquainted with that club would have known the rules. "Next time we'll eat there," he promised.

There wasn't a next time. The techno-plastics business his card loftily advertised turned out to involve cheap carnival prizes imported from Taiwan. If he would have been honest with me in the first place, it wouldn't have mattered that much.

Then there was Julian. He was handsome, friendly, intelligent, smooth, and came from a family whose name you would definitely recognize as being one of the wealthiest in the country. No one would have ever thought to question him or his credentials. In conversing with a few of his colleagues, however, I heard rumors of scandal, lawsuits, and personal bankruptcy. A quick trip to the courthouse told me everything I needed to know. Court records are available to the public, and if you know how to read them, you will be amazed at the wealth of information you can find. From those records I was able to discern this man's personal net worth, (under $1,000!), how much he ate, even how much he spent each month on dry-cleaning! It was a very different picture than the one he'd shown to my friends and me. Needless to say, from there I proceeded with extreme caution.

I learned how and where I could research these things from a friend of mine who works for a daily newspaper. She showed me how to read the records, which words were red flags, and which phrases would lead you to other, more detailed records. I would advise you to gain the same information from a reporter or an attorney friend of yours, and look things up before it gets too serious between you and your millionaire. You can never be too careful.

THE REAL THING

I hope that at this point I haven't made you so suspicious you want to give up. "Ain't nothing like the real thing, baby." Not everyone who appears to be wealthy is a conniving cur. There are many delightfully sincere gentlemen out there. How do you find them?

The best kinds of millionaires wear their wealth subtly. I remember meeting Jed as we worked together on a charity fund raiser. I had no idea he was wealthy. Sure, he seemed to know all the influential people in town, but he dressed horribly, drove an old V.W., and lived in a ratty duplex.

Jed and I became close friends. I knew he was an outdoorsman, so when my little brother came to town for a visit, I asked Jed to help me entertain him by taking him fishing. "Sure," Jed replied. "We'll just run up to the lake."

"The lake" turned out to be one of many belonging to the family business, which Jed helped run. It was situated on a ranch that was so beautiful and big it looked as if it should be declared a state park. It wasn't until then that I realized that Jed was somewhat above most of the rest of us on the economic scale.

Jed is generous and kind in every sense of the word. He spends money on others, just not on himself. The family funds are safe and multiplying in his hands. Now *that's* my idea of a millionaire. (Please don't write for his phone number or address. He is now happily and faithfully married).

Richard is another example. Physically, he's not a stand out. He's of average height, average build, wears expensive but average looking clothes. He's middle-aged and balding. No one would suspect at first that he was anything exceptional. But one day a group of us were dining in a restaurant that had a reputation for being the meeting place of the community's movers and shakers. As they passed by our table, each prominent person stopped by to warmly greet Richard, to shake his hand, to ask his advice. It was evident that this man was highly respected among his peers. They were practically paying homage to him. That was truly impressive.

When searching for a man of quality, you might try applying Harry Emerson Fosdick's definition of success. Does your man have these qualities?

"*To laugh often and much;*

To win the respect of intelligent people and the affection of children;

To earn the appreciation of honest critics and endure the betrayal of false friends;

To appreciate beauty;

To find the best in others;

To leave the world a bit better, whether by a healthy child, a garden patch, or a redeemed social condition;

> *To know even one life has breathed easier because*
>   *you lived.*
> *This is to have succeeded."*

If you can find a man who has succeeded on those terms, latch onto him with the fiercest grip you can muster. If he's wealthy, that's icing on the cake.

Discerning a man's monetary wealth is relatively easy, using the methods we've discussed. Discerning his wealth of character is a little more difficult. Watching how he is treated by his peers can be very useful.

Character references can also come from mutual friends. They say there are only six layers of separation between any of us, for example, "I know Marcus who knows Margarite who knows MacKenzie who knows your mother's manicurist." Do you see what I mean? Given time, if you live in the same city, you and your man can probably discover a mutual friend in far less than six layers. Use those channels to check up on him—subtly, of course.

Also, there are always a few people in every community who seem to know everybody. Get to know them. They will be just as happy to know you as you will be to know them. You expand their circle. And if that person doesn't know the man you're inquiring about, she will know someone else who does.

Ask that person about your man in a very casual way. You don't want it getting back to them that you are making inquiries. Say something like, "I ran into Burke Jolly the other day, and I just wanted you to know that he said some great things about you. He seems like a man who knows what he's talking about, does he?" That gives your friend an opening to tell you what she knows, without making her overly suspicious.

You must assure, however, that the people you ask are not A. women scorned, or B. business associates unhappy with the outcome of their negotiations.

"Antonio Triolo asked me out, but I don't know if I should get involved with him," a friend of mine told me. "Shelley Peterson used to date him, and told me she thought he was rather violently kinky."

That disturbed me, because Antonio was one of my closest friends, and I knew for a fact he was not this way at all. I also knew that he had taken Shelley out once and had not been interested past that. I think she resented it, and was acting accordingly.

I've also gotten bad character reports on men from associates whom I later learned had been legitimately beaten out for a certain position they were both competing for.

The best character references come from people you're sure are fairly objective, and from your own heart. If he says something that you're skeptical of, politely pin him down on it. Make him clarify it. Be sure you sound as if you're merely interested, rather than suspicious. For example, if he mentions that he's in the computer industry, ask him which company. If you have never heard of it, ask him what part of it he's involved in—engineering? Marketing? What? If he's truly involved, he'll warm to the subject and talk for at least a half-hour. If he's not involved, he'll give you vague, general answers that you can see right through, and he'll promptly change the subject.

The real secret to finding the quality ones is to look in quality places. When you search for good men, the rules are the same as in the search for good real estate. The most important things to consider are location, location, location.$

FIVE

Finding Prince Charming:
Where the Rich Boys Are

By now you've hopefully defined the kind of millionaire you're looking for. Your crusade will be greatly facilitated if you know the general vicinity in which to look. Just as you wouldn't shop for cornflakes at Nieman Marcus, you don't look for a millionaire in a bowling alley. Of course, there are some millionaires who like to bowl on occasion, but for the most part, if you go looking down at Lester's Bowl-O-Rama, you're going to find men with a penchant for polyester and for showing inappropriate cleavage while bending over the ball return.

To aid you in your quest, I've provided a list of places you're most likely to find a millionaire, and other places you're not likely to find them at all. There are exceptions, but remember, you can discern much about a millionaire by his environs:

Happy Hunting Grounds and the Rules For Using Them

The first-class section on airlines—This is ideal because if you're sitting in the first-class section as well, hopefully next to the single millionaire, conversation is unavoidable.

First-class is expensive, though. Try to use frequent flyer and promotional upgrades as much as possible. If the flight is full, tell the ticket agent you'd like to sit in first-class so they can sell your coach ticket to someone else. They often put coach passengers in first-class under these circumstances, so it might as well be you. I've done this many times. It's a roomier seat, and the food is much better.

Charity Work—This is hands-down the best and

most productive way to meet a millionaire. It's so important, in fact, that I've devoted a whole subdivision of this chapter to it. You'll get more on this later.

Country clubs—Most millionaires consider memberships to country clubs badges of honor, and belong to at least one.

A membership, however, is above and beyond most of our budgets, so the secret is to make friends with someone who has one. You'll be meeting wealthy women in your charity work. If they're members of a club, offer to play golf, tennis, racquetball, or swim with them. You can also offer to help at or with golf or tennis tournaments. Even if you live in a small town where wealthy men are few and far between, chances are you'll find them gathered at the one local country club.

Ski Resorts—There's a huge concentration of millionaires on the slopes. They fly in from all over the country to enjoy the finer resorts. My mother and I do our quickest and most productive harvesting here. While neither of us is a pro-skier, we both look pretty good in ski clothes, especially Mom, for a woman in her late 50's. Wealthy men appreciate the fact that at her age she's still out there schussing, and they can't resist skiing up and giving her a few tips, then offering to buy her lunch, espresso, whatever.

As for me, I know the areas around the resorts like the back of my hand, and offer that information liberally. Most men who have come in from out of town are grateful for the data, and often request that I accompany them, après ski, to the restaurants or clubs of my choice.

When attempting to meet men on the slopes we never, *never* innocently ski across their paths or gently ski into them, as some lunatics suggest. This is extremely angering and injurious, and could even bring about a lawsuit. Not a great way to make a first impression.

Instead, we try to position ourselves near the targeted man in the liftline, then strike up a conversation. If he is alone, my mother and I graciously split up so the interested party can double up with him on the chair. Then we have several minutes to chat with him exclusively until the ride ends.

Much of your success will depend on the resort you pick, and, unfortunately, the most productive are the most expensive. If you're flying to a resort for a weekend, skimp on accommodations (be vague about them when people ask), so you can splurge on lift tickets.

You don't have to have a huge wardrobe of ski outfits, either. One really nice suit will do, and can even be an asset to your identification if someone sees you one day and doesn't get the chance to approach you, but would like to find you the day after.

If you live in the area, see about season passes—they can offer you substantial discounts, and listen to the local media for discount promotions, which are frequently offered. I have been truly fortunate in this area. The dearest millionaire I know has extended the use of his ski passports to me, which entitle me to ski anywhere I want, anytime, completely gratis. I love treating Mom to a day on the slopes, and the passes usually end up being worth far more than the price of the tickets.

Expensive Restaurants. Find out which ones in your area are the favorites of the wealthy. That's easy enough to do by listening to the radio, local news programs, and by reading the society and gourmet pages of your local newspaper. Have breakfast or lunch there if you can't afford dinner. Go there often, with one or two friends who know the proper decorum but are not quite as attractive as you are. Note who dines there when, and try to be present when the men you're interested in are most likely to drop by.

After you've gone there several times with friends and have become a "regular," stop in at a provident time by yourself, and give your targeted millionaire the chance to approach *you*. Use all the techniques outlined later in this book for discreetly calling his attention to you, but do not directly approach him.

Never ask, even if he is alone, if you can join him. People are very peculiar about their eating habits, and generally have a planned mindset for how they should go. You will not fit in.

Besides, millionaires are used to being the ones who instigate things, the ones who conquer, and they have a hard time feeling as if they're being conquered themselves. It emasculates them and generally makes them suspicious. They're very cognizant of women who are after them for their money, and you don't want to be mistaken for one of those.

Exclusive shops. You know immediately that the men in these shops are probably well-off, or they wouldn't be buying there. If you're looking for a job, you could do worse than to seek employment in some of the spendier stores in their area. It gives you a chance to earn a living while passing time in the haunts of the wealthy, and you can't help but converse with them while they're there.

My friend Katy works in a prominent lighting store, of all places, and meets wealthy men every day as they come in to choose elegant fixtures for the houses they build or remodel. She's become somewhat of a lighting expert, and is often invited to their homes to consult with them about their lighting design. She meets at least one new, wealthy man each week.

If you already have a wonderful career somewhere else, drop in to these shops often. If you see a wealthy man with no wedding band deliberating over several objects, casually swing by and offer your positive opinion. "The tie on the left would look marvelous with your eyes," you could say as you move on. If he is interested in you or your opinion he will stop you with a comment like, "Do you really think so?" Or "Yes, but how do you think it would go with a camel cashmere blazer?"

Jewelry stores are exceptional places to meet wealthy men. You can get the most pertinent information about them in the shortest time. For example, if he's examining a piece of women's jewelry, you can say in passing, "That's a beautiful piece. I've been looking at it myself. I'm sure your girlfriend would be ecstatic to receive it." If it's not for his girlfriend but for his mother, sister, secretary, aunt, whatever, he will probably correct you. If he doesn't, he isn't interested and you can drop it right there. It's nothing personal, and you've lost nothing. But if he is interested, you've given him the perfect lead. He will appreciate this.

Certain health clubs. These are dicey, because the truly wealthy usually have personal trainers who come to visit them, or they work out on their own equipment at home. Still, there are some wealthy men who go to more exclusive health clubs to dabble at exercise while looking for hard-bodied women, or who are members of certain clubs because they are located close to their offices, making lunchtime or after-hours workouts convenient.

If you're going to join a health club, it might be worth your while to join a quality one near prosperous executive offices. Go by there several times before you join to see which types of men frequent the place. Don't be fooled or distracted by the lusciously muscle-bound. If they're extremely well chiseled, chances are they're spending at least three hours a day on their bodies, and most millionaires don't have that kind of time to spend on exercise.

When you think about it, who does? If they took two of those hours per day and spent them helping underprivileged children, they'd accomplish so much more than superbly sculptured forms. Don't get caught in that trap yourself.

One of the reasons health clubs offer more limited possibilities for getting to know wealthy men is that you will very likely get lost in a sea of better bodies than yours. Your ego doesn't need that. Also, if you're working hard, you're not at your pristine best. Sweat, strain, and grimaces don't always show you off to your best advantage. On the other hand, if you put on makeup, designer workout clothes, and try too hard to stay pretty, you'll look ridiculous and won't fool anybody.

If it's a good workout you seek, however, go for it, then freshen up afterward and hit the spa's health food bar, where interesting men are probably congregating. It might be worth a shot.

Sporting Events. You'll find the wealthy men in the best seats, enjoying the game and the social parade that goes along with professional sports. Unfortunately, it's hard for us to get access to that. Most of us don't want to invest the kind of money it would take for season tickets near the elite, and even if we were willing to spend it, those tickets are generally not available.

But don't despair! This is where your wealthy friends can help again. God bless my financial adviser! I don't invest that much with him, but he still lets me use his season tickets several times a season, and I've met some very interesting people in those seats. I was even stopped once, several nights after I'd used them, by a man who said, "I saw you in Phil's seats at the game the other night. I sit right below him. Are you a basketball fan? Maybe we could go to a game some time." He didn't have to ask twice. I pinned him down right then and there.

You can also score free tickets by becoming a valued customer of a business that uses their season tickets and boxes for promotional purposes, a little like my financial adviser. Banks, insurance companies, medical corporations and others often have boxes, and sometimes have drawings for seats, as do radio stations. Try for them every chance you get.

You will be surprised what is available to you if you're resourceful. A good friend of mine who is wealthy in wit called recently, and inquired if I liked professional baseball. When I assured him that I did, he informed me that his mother was a receptionist for one of the businesses owned by an extremely prominent entrepreneur in town. He owned a box, and frequently gave the extra tickets to employees. His mother had gotten her hands on four of them. Would I like to come with them? Would I? I had a great time in the box that night, and met some very interesting people. I would have been a fool not to take advantage of the situation. You need to cultivate situations like these.

If, when all is said and done, you have no way of getting tickets in the really good sections, you and your friends can buy cheap tickets, then run down between quarters or at the half and buy concessions in the areas adjacent to the better sections. People are usually quite congenial during breaks, and a positive comment about a particular play in passing might score you some points with a potential teammate.

Political campaigns. Make yourself invaluable to a candidate, and you are sure to have exposure to many of his or her wealthy supporters. It is to the rich man's advantage to be politically active—politicians' decisions often affect his wealth, so he will be found contributing both time and money to ensure the candidates of his choice are elected. Plus, there is a certain amount of prestige involved in attending big-ticket fund raisers, and the wealthy man is a sucker for prestige.

The more prestigious the fund raising event, the more the ticket per plate is likely to cost, and this might be off limits to you. I personally can't justify spending $500 on a dinner, no matter how strongly I feel about the cause it's supporting. I do have friends, however, whose companies buy entire tables at these events, and they often have to scramble to fill one or two seats at the table. They know they can count on me to fill in at the last minute, dressed appropriately, well informed, and well behaved.

I also have many married female friends who know they can implicitly trust me with their husbands, so when they are sick or out of town, they'll call and ask me to be the other half of the couple their husband has committed to. These situations are perfect. Everyone knows I'm not attached to my escort, and they're more than eager to introduce me to the eligible men in the room. It would behoove you to develop these kinds of relationships. I've found them very gratifying.

It's beneficial as well to get involved in the actual hands-on work that's involved in a campaign. In a recent gubernatorial race, I found a few typos in some of the press releases of a candidate I admired, so I promptly went down to his campaign office and offered my services as an editor, writer, and proof reader. He was so grateful he immediately made me a member of his inner-circle of supporters, and at their meetings I met a multitude of wealthy single men—also wealthy married men with single brothers and sons. Our candidate didn't win, but I certainly did. My social calendar was filled for months afterward thanks to those leads.

Major artistic events. On opening and closing nights of operas, plays, or art exhibits, galas or receptions are often held. Special invitations usually go out to major patrons or season ticket holders, but they are sometimes open to the public as well, for a price. Ask about it at the box office when you purchase your tickets, which, to be on the safe side, you should do well in advance. Also, as a volunteer for the fund raising arm of that specific organization, you are sure to be able to finagle an invitation. These are invaluable venues for meeting millionaires.

Appropriate clothing is essential for these kinds of events. You must look elegant, yet interesting. Pull out your basic black dress and accessorize. Make sure you feel comfortable, sexy, gorgeous.

Topics of conversation are obvious at these

events—you discuss the artwork or the performances. Of course you'll have read and retained the information on the program notes, and if you had time before you came, you will have read reviews and other information that pertains to that particular production. Looking great and armed with insightful comments, you're ready to seek out your prey.

Occasionally millionaires will attend these events unescorted, but not often. Just because they're with a woman doesn't mean they're off limits, however. If they're with a woman and they're wearing wedding rings, or if they're with a woman and being openly affectionate, leave them alone. They belong to someone else for the evening, and you wouldn't want anyone whom you could easily distract.

However, many times millionaires will attend these events with relatives or friends. I often go escorted by millionaires with whom I have platonic relationships, and we're of great mutual benefit to each other. They introduce me to their eligible friends, and I get them information about the women they see who look interesting to them. The woman at the millionaire's side may actually be a scout who could be your greatest ally. If you see a couple that appears to be in this situation, approach them and speak to the female first. That way you'll make a favorable impression on both parties, and never be accused of invading anyone's territory.

Wealthy neighborhoods. You have to take your clothes to the cleaner somewhere—why not drop them off at a cleaner in a luxurious neighborhood, if it's not too far from where you live or not too expensive. Servants don't always pick up the laundry—a millionaire in a pinch will gather his himself. Buy your gas in expensive neighborhoods. Do your shopping there. Jog or ride your bike there, for heaven's sake. If you get enough positive exposure, men will be approaching you. Get into a routine. See if you can't make it match the routine of the men you find interesting.

If you're looking for a new place to live and can't afford a home in these luxurious areas, check on the possibility of renting a carriage house apartment or mother-in-law cottage behind one of the elegant homes. Sometimes these are reserved for servants, but they're often open to a responsible and neat outside renter. It is difficult to find a situation like this in the newspaper, so you might have to do some legwork on your own through the neighborhoods of your choice. Living conditions like theses are ideal, since you'll be on the same streets and blocks with wealthy men every day of your life. It's far more productive, and maybe even less expensive, than living in a large apartment complex on the other side of town.

I have very fond memories of the summer Natalie rented a poolhouse behind an elegant home in an upscale neighborhood outside Los Angeles. I was a constant visitor, and we met all sorts of interesting men as we walked her dogs down the street. Waiting for our take-out at the local gourmet pizzeria was like attending a "Who's Who" convention. Natalie and I were very busy that summer.

Supermarkets in expensive neighborhoods. As sexist as this may sound, many men are still bewildered infants when it comes to grocery shopping. Wealthy single men fall victim to this more than average single men, because the rich have usually had someone else to do their shopping and cooking for them. Still, sometimes they get a craving or run out of something essential on the help's day off, and they can be found pushing their carts down those supermarket aisles, just waiting for some kind soul to rescue them. The produce section is best, because raw fruits and vegetables can be very intimidating.

If you see a well-dressed man standing forlornly in the vegetable aisle, push your cart past him and cheerfully say, "Those mushrooms are incredible if you sauté them in butter and splash in a little white wine." Or make some other epicurean comment about the nearest vegetable at hand. This will not only relieve him of his current dilemma, but will impress him with the fact that you know how to cook. Many millionaires are especially susceptible to a home-cooked meal for reasons we will discuss later, and you will have made a favorable impression right off the bat.

Alumnae functions. If you live anywhere near a prestigious university and are looking for a job, check first with that university's alumnae association for full-time work planning events, fund raisers, or even doing clerical work. So many wealthy men are proud of the institutions that helped make them what they are today, and continue to support the schools through their alumnae programs. Related jobs can give you priceless exposure, and access to detailed background information on a plethora of wealthy men.

If you can't find work with one of these organizations, see if you can get one of your well-educated buddies to take you to his class-reunion or alumnae activities. He'll need an attractive and stimulating companion to show off, and you'll be able to discreetly collect leads. One of these days I'm going to convince my friend Olivio to take me back to Yale with him for the class reunion he attends every year. My mouth waters at the prospects.

Polo matches. There isn't a polo club in every community, but where there is, there are single men with money. In many areas, polo matches have become quite the yuppie event. Only the extremely wealthy participate, because it's an incredibly expensive sport to get involved with. But if you know a bit about the sport and dress appropriately, you're bound to meet interesting people at the matches.

To truly enjoy them, do a few reconnaissance missions first. Go very inconspicuously, almost in disguise, to the first few matches, and observe what people are doing, saying, how they're dressing, and how they're acting. Once you're confident in that situation, put on your best polo clothes and your happiest smile, and go back in full-glory. No one will even recognize you from before. There's something very dashing about watching grown men ride around on ponies while they chase a tiny ball, and they will esteem a woman who appreciates that. A smile and a casual comment like, "Beautiful play," could win you a polo player's heart forever.

Expensive vacation resorts. You have to be careful here because many men who are not so well-off will scrape together their last dimes for a week at Club Med or other such resorts. They hope to snag a rich woman who will support them. By the time you master everything in the first several chapters of this book, you will be exuding class and elegance, and these vipers will likely make you their target. Just as in a vacation setting they have no way to check up on you, you will have no way to check up on them. Move extremely cautiously.

Also, when people are in an exotic location far from home, they tend to make promises they can't keep, or have no intention of keeping. Sure, you'll find millionaires there, but they're likely to be in the vacation mode where anything goes. I wouldn't set my sites on any long-term relationships with the men you meet there. Oh, they do happen. I have one North American friend who met the Mexican woman he would eventually marry while they were both on vacation in Cancun. But that is definitely the exception. Most of the promises made on vacation don't even carry over to the next day, let alone to when you're back home in your own element.

Julia learned this the hard way. "Wake up, everybody!" She told us as she bounced merrily into the hotel room we shared in Acapulco. "I met a great guy at the disco last night who has invited us all out to his yacht for breakfast. We set sale at 8:00. Get moving!" We groaned, because we'd been out dancing until about 5:00 that morning. Still, the prospect of breakfast on a yacht was appealing, so we rolled out of bed, put ourselves together, and grabbed a taxi for the marina, where her friend said he'd be waiting for us. You guessed it. No friend. Julia hadn't been perceptive enough to ask the name of the yacht, if he truly had one, or even the last name of the millionaire. She felt foolish for having believed him, and for getting the rest of us out of bed at that ungodly hour. We forgave her, however. It got us to a part of the resort town we'd never before seen.

On one vacation, I was even guilty of making promises I couldn't keep. There was just something in the air. Those declarations of affection I made on a balmy night in Tenerife seemed absolutely preposterous once I returned to the states. The situation resulted in the monstrous wrath and phone bill of an irate and frustrated, but very handsome Canary Islander. I felt foolish, callous, and frivolous. I wouldn't do it again.

So, there really is absolutely nothing wrong with meeting wealthy men at expensive vacation resorts, it's just not wise to make any promises to them, or take anything they say to you seriously. Go out there to enjoy yourself and have a good time, but not to seek anything of depth or permanence.

BUT THE GREATEST OF THESE IS CHARITY

I have to devote several pages to charity work, because your involvement with it will be far and away the most productive time you spend. The kinds of millionaires you will meet in these situations are, for the most part, socially and community conscious. Beware the man who amasses large amounts of money and is too busy counting it or spending it to contribute time or funds to charitable causes.

Through community service, you'll get the chance to work with wealthy men on a personal, heart-to-heart level that you won't find at clubs or parties. You can let them be impressed by your efficiency and dedication, qualities that are truly admirable, and you can be impressed by their commitment and compassion. Working together to accomplish a worthy goal is a great way to become acquainted with someone on more than just the surface level.

And even if you don't meet a millionaire through your community service (though the chances are slim that you won't), these projects will bring you tremendous personal satisfaction. You'll become a more complete person. You might even play an active roll in saving someone's life, which is far more fulfilling than securing dates with the wealthy.

Now there are several rules to which you should adhere when doing volunteer work. Your efforts will be of little use if you don't stick faithfully to these guidelines:

1. Always arrive on time to meetings and events.
2. Be committed to spending at least several hours per week per cause.
3. Volunteer for as many projects as you can successfully accommodate.
4. Don't bite off more than you can chew. If you can't finish it, don't say you'll start it.
5. Don't skip meetings. Notify others if an emergency comes up and it is impossible for you to attend.
6. Document all your efforts. Keep careful track of them.

7. Don't procrastinate. Finish your assignments as soon as possible.

8. Don't be afraid to ask for help. If there are full-time employees working for the organization, helping you is part of their job.

9. Be courteous, warm, and helpful to everyone involved.

10. Research the organization. Do your homework. The people you approach will be asking you questions, and you need to have ready answers.

MY TOP FOUR

I've been involved in a vast number of fund raising and community service projects, but for our purposes here, I will tell you about the four that have been most productive man-wise. Let me assure you that I originally became involved in these causes because I believe in them. If your interest is not sincere and your only motive for helping is millionaire exposure, you will betray yourself and look mercenary and foolish. It shouldn't be too hard to find a cause you truly feel good about supporting.

160

FUND RAISING FOR MEDICAL CAUSES

Some of my most rewarding experiences have come through work with the Cystic Fibrosis Foundation. I had friends with children who suffered from this almost always fatal disease, and I was eager to help them with research fund raising projects. Through this foundation, I assisted in organizing athletic events, receptions, luncheons, and a few "Bid for Bachelor" programs that were especially fun and productive.

Can you imagine a better excuse to call your area's most eligible men? "Hello," I'd say, "I'm L.A. Johnson, a volunteer with the Cystic Fibrosis Foundation. Our annual "Bid for Bachelors" is coming up, and your name has been submitted as one of the most attractive men in the city. Would you be interested in participating? What? You'd like to discuss it over lunch? Why of course. When would be convenient for you?"

They are so flattered to be considered among the most attractive men in the community that even if they're too shy to participate in the event, they almost always make a large contribution. We used those funds for "insurance money" for other bachelors. That meant that if no one was bidding on someone, I would bid, using the money donated by others. The bachelors I bought would never know, and would have the satisfaction of being sold at a decent price. I would have the satisfaction of going on an elaborate date with a prominent man without having to spend more than I could afford. There is no way anyone can lose with a project like this.

My work with Cystic Fibrosis has been fantastic for me because not only have I felt as if I've been helping my friends, but the research in this field has brought doctors tantalizingly close to a cure. I would encourage you to get involved with any organization that raises funds for the cure of any disease that touches you. There are hundreds of organizations out there. Look in your phonebook, or call city hall and tell them you would like to spend some time volunteering. They will be delighted to hear from you, and will give you a long list of people who need help.

FINE ARTS SUPPORT GROUPS

The second organization that has offered me particularly rewarding involvement is the Symphony Guild. I got involved with this one when the associate conductor, who I was seeing at the time, explained to me how most symphonies cannot survive on the revenue of retail ticket sales alone. They're in desperate need of contributions from the community. Most fine arts companies are, and I'd advise you to get involved in fund raising to support them. Do you like modern dance? Ballet? Opera? Theater? If not, try your best to develop a taste for at least one, and become an integral part of its fund raising arm.

When I first joined the Symphony Guild, my motives were altruistic, but it didn't take me long to start realizing the social advantages. Granted, the membership was mostly older and female, but those older females had sons, nephews and friends. It also gave me access to touring guest performers and members of the board of directors, which is made up of some prominent and attractive community leaders.

I began to receive invitations to galas, receptions, and balls that were just teeming with wealthy men. They are the financial backbones of the artistic community. All I had to do was pay my dues and appear at these functions well dressed and smiling. Men would actually seek me out, thanks to the promptings they'd received from my fellow committee members who had been impressed by my diligence and my adherence to the ten rules I've previously mentioned.

It can work like this: Sitting at a board meeting

(I'm on the board now), we all listened politely as a man from a large department store chain based in my city explained how the Symphony Guild would help them sponsor a huge anniversary banquet and benefit performance. Every prominent person in the state was to be invited. Unfortunately, the ticket price would be a tremendous strain on my meager budget. "Now I'll have to find someone interesting to take me," I sighed to the well-dressed woman on my right. "Let me see…" she pondered. "I know! Chet DeVore! He's a vice-president over at Darnell and Thomas. He lost his wife a while ago. Let me arrange a meeting for you two!" This woman was a mover and shaker herself. Soon Chet DeVore was happily whisking me off in his golden Mercedes convertible.

My friend Carlotta has also inadvertently found another avenue of exposure to wealthy men via her patronage of the fine arts—and it's tax deductible! She makes a sizable donation to a certain performing group every year, and that gives her access to a poshly appointed room full of wine, hors d'oeuvres, and wealthy men, during the intermission of each performance. Although the motives for her donation were purely in support of the ensemble, she can't deny the contact it gives her with some of the community's most elite. Check the program they give you at the performance for lists of donor's benefits, and discern if they would be worth your while.

In a brief aside from volunteerism, but keeping with the theme of fine arts, I can't stress enough how fertile they'll be in your pursuit of a millionaire. Attach yourself to the fine arts, and you can't help but get exposure to the wealthy.

Angie is a great example of this. While working her way through college, she took a job at the symphony box office. It was the smartest move she ever made.

"Julio," I called out to one of my millionaire friends as I passed him in the hall of our condo complex. "You're going to the symphony anniversary concert and dinner tonight, aren't you? Everyone who's anyone will be there. It's a very important event." Julio had recently acquired his fortune (legally, of course), and had asked me to coach him on improving his social standing in the community.

"But I don't have a date!" he cried. "Where can I get one at this hour?"

"I'll see what I can do," I replied, mentally scouring my list of appropriate friends. "Just run down to the box office and pick up the best tickets you can get. We'll deal with the date issue later."

It seems we never had to. Julio met Angie at the box office, and exchanged his heart for the tickets. He took her to the concert and dinner, and to my surprise, I saw them together again the very next night, at a benefit for our sister state in Africa. They've been together ever since. They're married now, blissfully raising children and spending at least half the year abroad.

WORKING WITH TEENAGERS

Another of the most satisfying, fulfilling, and productive community service projects I've been involved in is my work at the juvenile detention center. I drive over and do cooking or art projects with the "guests" out there, or I play various sports with them—everything from kite flying to Frisbee golf to softball. I'll admit that I haven't met one millionaire through this, but my experiences have given me some fascinating tales to tell at parties, and I can discover much about the men I date from whether or not they're willing to accompany me on an activity night and help me with the kids.

Then there's the moral support the kids themselves give me. One night, dressed in our evening finery, my affluent escort and I had finished our après theater dinner and began the two-block trek back to my condo. We were suddenly accosted by some very rough-looking teenagers sporting tattoos, earrings, weapons, and other sundry gang attire. My date turned pale and began to sweat and shake. One of the gang members stepped menacingly toward me. He was a kid I'd tagged out on third in a softball game at the detention center the week before.

"Yo, L.A.!" he said, his face breaking into a smile. "Who's the dude? He treatin' you right?"

Those kids won for me that man's undying admiration, and he still tells that story at all the social and family gatherings we attend.

While it's not always opportune to have a young prostitute, dressed to score, run up to you on the street and throw her arms around you (which I've had happen), I'll take the camaraderie those kids give me any day. If I can be of assistance to them, I can be of assistance to anyone.

WORKING WITH CHILDREN

Along those lines is one other small, community service-oriented project that I should mention, not only because of the great fulfillment it provides, but because I'd probably have severely bruised shins if I failed to note it. I taught a Sunday School class full of rambunctious six- and seven-year-olds. None of their fathers are single millionaires, but this work was very beneficial to me in other ways.

A woman in my life situation doesn't get much contact with children, but my class gives me invaluable experience for the times one of the wealthy men I'm seeing suddenly springs a son or a niece on me. I know exactly how to handle them.

Besides, my position as a Sunday School teacher lends me an aura of respect in certain conservative circles, and many wealthy circles are conservative— that's how they earned their money in the first place. "Mother, I'd like to introduce you to L.A. She teaches children in Sunday School." Can you believe I've been introduced that way more than once? It's always met with a very warm reception among Protestants and the like. I usually forget to mention this to the Jews or Muslims I become involved with. The WASPish men I see know I'm not like any Sunday School teacher they ever had, but it goes a long way with the parents. Any volunteerism with your chosen religion can be a positive.

It may sound painfully puritanical, but even men who don't believe in organized religion have been very supportive of my efforts with the kids. I find them, of their own accord, picking up gifts, treats and visual aids for my class. They won't usually admit it, but they like the little rugrats as much as I do, and they love hearing about their antics.

And lastly, I believe that God hears and answers the prayers of small children. My class doesn't quite understand a mommy-aged person like me without a corresponding daddy-aged person. So every week they pray, "please help our teacher find a nice man she'll want to marry." I figure it can't hurt.

NOT-SO-HAPPY HUNTING GROUNDS

It's not that millionaires *never* go to these places, it's just that they're so hard to siphon out from the rest of the decidedly non-millionaire element that you'd probably be wasting your time. Also, in some of these places wealthy men wouldn't admit their true identities. Don't bother with places like:

Laundromats
Bowling alleys
Wal-Marts
Warehouse stores
Video arcades
Tractor pulls
Denny's
Truck stops
Adult magazine shops

Cafeterias

Pawn shops

Bus stations

Outlet malls

Roller skating rinks

Professional wrestling matches

Miniature golf courses

Male or female strip clubs

Classified personal ads

Belly-dancing recitals

Cosmetology school

Auto parts stores. $

SIX

Making the Connection: Catching His Eye

Even though you're in all the right places at all the right times, if the millionaires don't notice you, you might as well be stuck alone in an elevator.

Ideally, someone has already caught your millionaire's eye for you. A mutual friend has told him all sorts of wonderful things about you, and he is just dying to meet you. Unfortunately, that is not often the way it happens. You're more frequently in a room with 'the man' and a hundred other people, and you're left to your own devices.

We've already discussed some ways for you to get his attention—by wearing elegant, interesting, and appropriate clothes, and by making positive, helpful comments in the right setting. But you want more than his attention. You want his *desire*. You want to inspire him to follow you home, to call you tomorrow, to send you flowers the next day, and to start inviting you on sumptuous adventures. How do you motivate that?

THE SUBLIMINAL "OH BABY! OH BABY!"

Most *femme fatales* can't put their fingers exactly on what they do to make men fall at their feet, but my friend Lauren, ever brilliant and eloquent, sums it up quite nicely.

Lauren is the first to admit that her looks are not her strong point. Although she has good taste in clothes, she's slightly overweight, and none of her features are particularly outstanding. They never have been, but no one ever noticed that. She's been knocking them dead for as long as I've known her, since she was about seven. She's always been able to have any man she wanted, and she's always had to fight off the many men she doesn't want.

We were discussing this one day, in a club over warm lobster salads that would go on one of her rich friends' tabs. "It's simple," she said, revealing her secret. "You make eye contact, then you give them the subliminal, 'Oh baby! Oh baby!'"

"Oh baby! Oh baby?" I asked, laughing. "What do you meant by that?"

"Just watch," she said as the waiter approached. At the time Lauren was a 34-year-old attorney, divorced, with four kids at home. The waiter was a hunky college student, about 22. Lauren made eye contact with him, then gave him that look that said, "Oh baby! Oh baby! You're the hottest thing I've ever seen and we need each other *bad*!"

Within seconds that waiter was practically sitting in her lap. He couldn't be attentive enough, and even brought us free dessert. Lauren ate her brandied mousse with a smug smile on her face, and said, "I told you it was simple."

Many women do this, they just don't explain it as eloquently as Lauren does. My friend Irene used to label it "Calling him with your eyes." We'd go to dance clubs in a very affluent section of town, make eye-contact with interesting men, and see who could get a man to cross the room to us first. Practice this. Millionaires, waiters, men from all walks of life fall hopeless victims to it, unless they're sick, preoccupied, gay, or near-sighted. This method is indispensable, especially when there's no one around to provide an introduction for you.

First Impressions

Once you've got his attention with the "subliminal Oh baby! Oh baby!," however, you'll need to have something to say to him. A great lead will die if you have nothing to follow it up. Your first comment should be something positive, and a little bizarre.

Society is so negative today, and we're often tempted to make derogatory observations. "These affairs are such a bore!" might be words that come to your mind. Don't let them pass your lips. Think of something more positive, something more original.

As ridiculous as it may sound, Abby always uses lines from famous poetry, especially *The Jabberwocky*, by Lewis Carroll. "It's brillig in these slithy toves," she'll say with a twinkle in her eye, and the millionaire is instantly intrigued. "I'm embarrassed to admit that I didn't have a clue as to what she was talking about," said one of her wealthy victims. "But the words sounded vaguely familiar, and I thought, 'here's a woman with a playful vocabulary. Let's see what else she has to say.'" The more literary men are impressed with her poetic references.

That's one way to spark an interest. The object of your first contact with these men, however, is to make a favorable, memorable impression, then leave. Don't linger. It can grow awkward when two people who don't know each other are forced to converse for any length of time. Make your impression, chat for a few brief minutes, then, without cutting him off, move on. If he's interested, he'll find you again before the end of the event that brought you together.

Here's an example of how this works. A few years ago, a prominent entertainer came to town, and I spotted him at the concert a mutual friend was giving. He was alone and looking slightly out of place. Just before the concert began, I casually walked up to him, gave him 'the look,' told him we were happy to have him in our city, and I hoped that he would enjoy the concert. I then walked away. He approached me a few minutes later, patting his pockets, obviously searching for some object.

"Did you misplace something?" I asked.

"Yes," he replied. "I don't seem to have a pen,

and I'd like to take notes. You wouldn't happen to have something I could borrow, would you?"

"I'm sure I do," I replied, as I began digging through my purse. I was about to hand him a ballpoint, when I spied, sitting next to it, a tube of new, bright red lipstick. "I'm afraid this is all I have, but you're welcome to use it," I said as I slowly uncapped it and provocatively extended it with a lascivious twist.

"Th-th-th-thank you!" he stammered as he took the proffered object. A smile and a blush crept across his face, but when he looked up, I was gone and the concert was about to begin.

After the program, it didn't surprise me one bit that he came rushing up to me, lipstick in hand, along with his card. "Please come backstage to see me after one of my performances," he implored. "I can arrange for tickets if you'd like. I'd really enjoy seeing you again."

Be on your toes when you're making that first impression. Zap him, then move on.

If you do it right, he'll come and find you for the next encounter.

HAVING WORDS

During your second contact with him, when he approaches you because you've intrigued him, you must make him feel comfortable, at ease. He needs to know that if he were to spend more time with you, it could be an exciting yet facile experience. I've provided you a list of do's and don'ts for your first conversation with a man of means. It can save you from some fatal mistakes:

DO TALK ABOUT:	DON'T TALK ABOUT:
Him!	*Your ex*
Local sports events	*His ex*
Local fine arts	*Money*
Current, tasteful jokes	*Problems with your children*
His family	*Problems with your weight*
His work	*Problems with his weight*
Your work (make it sound interesting)	*Your health*
What's going on around	*Personal problems*
Interesting places to which you've both traveled	*Other dates*
Food	*Your age*

His attire	His age
Interesting articles you've read that pertain to mutual interests	Your attire
The stock market	Unflattering facts about mutual friends
Observations about other people	Domestic chores
The weather	Local politics
Interesting movies, plays, or books	Plastic surgery
Recent changes in anything	Death

HE'LL GET YOUR NUMBER

Once you've captivated him with your sparkling conversation, it's important for you to make sure he knows where he can find you, or requests that you find him. The first contact you casually instigated and cut short, now he has come back for more. Make sure he gets it.

Don't do anything as crass as offering him your phone number. If he's interested, he'll ask. Don't despair if he doesn't, however. He might think that's a little too blatant, and instead he'll ask you for your full name, so he can look you up in the directory, or he'll ask the specific name of your work place, so he can find you there. If you find him interesting and think he can be trusted, make sure he gets the information he needs to approach you later. Chat about mutual friends, so he'll understand he can contact you through them.

With men you're wary of, however, be careful not to give out any specific information at all. Be extremely vague. When he asks your name, merely give him your first name. When he asks where you work, just say give the vicinity, like "downtown," or "on the East Side." If he asks where you live, tell him, "in an apartment," or "in a house." Never give out false information, however. You might later discover that this man is worthwhile after all, or that he has some very worthwhile friends. You wouldn't want your first interaction with him to be full of deceit.

It's important to act wisely, to play it cool in the embryonic stages of a relationship. On first meeting, keep the conversation light, positive, and clever. Give him the impression that associating with you would be a much needed breath of fresh air. Don't reveal all there is to know about yourself—make him feel that you're a provocative mystery, waiting to be solved.

If he's given you his card, wait at least three days

to call him. Don't despair if he waits a little longer to get in touch with you. Wealthy men are often very busy. It could take him as long as two weeks. Any longer than that, don't get your hopes up. Continue working on others. But then again, don't be surprised if there's a message from this one waiting for you when you get to the office the next day. It's very probable that you've left the man simmering, at the point of boiling over, "like water for chocolate." It will be up to you to know how to turn the heat up or down. That's a great art I'm about to teach you.$

SEVEN
Care and Feeding of a Millionaire: Keeping Him on the Line

Oh, so he called you, did he? Don't be so surprised. You've done everything right so far. Keep up the good work. If the man is as exciting as your initial impression indicates, you'll want to keep him coming back after the first date. There are all sorts of things you can do to encourage this. I have a friend who has this down pat.

My friend's name is Stan, and I fell for everything he did. I don't think I've ever seen anyone maneuver so adroitly to get a second, third, fourth . . . well, let's face it, we dated for six months. Even though I'm not a millionaire male, I associate with so many of them that my tastes are quite similar, and what worked with me can easily work with them. This is what happened:

I met Stan briefly at a party, and discovered that he was trying to lease out a spacious condominium in my building. Since I had another wealthy friend who'd ask me to alert him if anything opened up, I gave Stan my card and told him to call me as soon as he'd redecorated the place and it was ready to be shown. It was one of those parties where the men were legion, and I was constantly distracted. I didn't give Stan a second thought.

So I was surprised and somewhat puzzled when Stan gave me a call at my office about a week later. "The condo is all set to be shown," he said. "Would you like to see it first, so you'll know whether or not to recommend it to your friend?"

"Sure," I said distractedly. "But I'm leaving town this week. Can you call me next week?"

"Of course," he replied, and he did. But this time he asked if, after he'd shown me the condo, would I be interested in playing racquetball on the building's courts?

Racquetball? I thought. Where did that come from? How did he know I liked to play racquetball? Oh well. Why not? Willing partners at my level are hard to find. (I'm not very good).

He showed up at the appointed hour with a lily. Nothing inappropriately romantic like a rose or a bouquet, just a single flower. He was very patient and positive with me as we played, and subtly asked me many questions, finding out my interests and quirks. We discovered we both adored mountain sports, and that I love trying new things. "I'll be going snowshoeing soon," he told me. "If you've never been, you'll have to try it. I'll let you know when I go, and you can come along." He then left with no kiss, hug, or handshake. "What a nice guy," I thought as he walked down the hall.

I was a little surprised when he called two days later to set the up the activity. We had a great time, he went out of his way to make sure I was well equipped and comfortable, and at the end of the date he lightly kissed me on the lips. The electricity there surprised us both. "Oh!" he exclaimed. "That was really nice. I'll call you again—soon."

Stan used all the right tricks on me. Let's analyze them, and turn them around so you can use them on someone like him.

When we first met at the party, Stan established a common cause (leasing his condo), and found an excuse to call. He didn't become overly eager by calling me immediately, but waited until he had a good reason. He also didn't become put off because I delayed things for another week. In the meantime he did his homework. He found out from mutual friends that I liked sports and exotic flowers.

During the first date, he asked questions, established more common interests, and used them to lure me on a second date. He was not at all pushy.

On the second date he showed me what a good companion he could be. With the light kiss he titillated me, giving me hints of exciting things to come.

You can do all these things and more. Here's a little list to help get you two on your way. I must caution you, however, don't use them all at once on the same person. That might overwhelm him. Select those actions which are most appropriate for your millionaire, then spread them out:

1. On your first date, *establish common interests, and express great enthusiasm for them*. You also might express appreciation for the fact that he enjoys doing things so few others have the taste, courage, sense of

adventure, or whatever, to try. This will let him know that your partner options for this particular activity are limited, and that you would really appreciate enjoying it with him. Try something like, "Are you kidding? You like Brazilian music? So few people around here can really appreciate it! Have you ever heard it at the Rio?"

2. *Be positive, but not Polly Anna-ish*. Glen took Danielle out for the first time, and came back "hyperglycemic." "Everything I said I liked, she clapped her hands and told me she just loved," he said. "At first I liked the fact that she wasn't negative, but by the end of the evening I told her I liked eating head cheese on rye while sitting naked in a plastic wading pool, just to see what she'd say. As I suspected, she thought it would be a kick."

3. During your first outing with him, *let him know that you lead a lively and vibrant life*. You're a woman in demand, not just by other men, but by organizations, business associates, and your family. Chances are he'll want to be a part of some of that vibrancy.

4. *Don't sound too vibrant or busy.* You don't want him to think you'll never have time to fit him in, or that everything else comes before an interesting relationship.

5. *Don't forget to tell him that you had a good time, and to thank him.* This is only polite.

6. *Make sure all the lines of connection between you two are clear.* If he enjoys the first date, he might want to find out what other people think of you, for some positive reinforcement. Be sure you're in good standing with all your mutual acquaintances. If there is someone who knows both of you and has a negative impression, call that person, and without mentioning your millionaire, try to make amends.

7. *Do some homework of your own.* If you know someone who knows him well, find things out about him that he hasn't yet had a chance to tell you. Is there a particular perfume he loves? Is he allergic to anything? Is there a certain flavor he relishes or abhors? Use this information to surprise him next time you see him.

8. During your initial outings, *be lightly affectionate but not overly passionate.* As you get to know each other, your passion will have a better foundation. Too much too quickly could easily scare a millionaire off. Give him something to come back for.

9. *Wait a day or two after a date, then send him a clever thank-you note.* When I'm at art museums, I usually pick up interesting and bizarre art print notecards. I now have quite a collection, and I always have on hand something playful that specifically pertains to something amusing the millionaire said or did.

10. *Don't become over-anxious and waste time and effort worrying if he doesn't call you back immediately.* Most millionaires are busy men, and often place personal gratification behind business gratification. His business might get the best of him for a while. But you can do very subtle things to convey to him the fact that you still exist.

11. *Let a mutual friend know you had a good time, but don't gush.* This will get back to him, and give him the signal that you'd like to see him

again. Millionaires may be extremely successful in their chosen fields, but they're often a little nervous when it comes to affairs of the heart. Some positive reinforcement couldn't hurt.

12. During the course of your new relationship, *if you see an article that he would find interesting or amusing, Xerox it and send him a copy.* If other matters have become more pressing in his life than your relationship, this will give him a little reminder that you are still around, as savvy and supportive as ever.

13. *Let him know you can be spontaneous!* That way, if something wonderful comes up at the last minute, he won't hesitate to call you. Of course, you don't want to sound too available, but if he suddenly finds he has the opportunity to attend the Academy Awards and would like you to accompany him, tell him, for an event like that, you certainly could change your plans.

14. *If something interesting in your life comes up and you need an escort, you would not be out of line to call and invite him to join you.* My season symphony tickets afford me wonder-

ful excuses to invite interesting men along. "Hi, Ben!" I'll say after I've been out with him two or three times, "I have these tickets for the symphony Friday night. Christopher Parkening will be playing with them, and it should be wonderful." That works divinely. They'll almost always offer to take you out to dinner before or after the concert. As a matter of fact, it will reflect poorly on them if they don't.

15. Last, but not least, I'm sure this sounds disgustingly insidious, but it has been known to work. If all signals are positive, *leave something of yours in his car, pocket, or home.* I'm ashamed to admit it, but my earrings and lipstick have probably been "forgotten" in 49 of the 50 states. (I've never been to Alaska.) Know that your millionaire will probably see right through it, and he will either be flattered or cynical. Flattery never hurts, and if he's cynical about it, he's probably not too interested anyway. Getting the item back either gives you a chance to set another date, or to acknowledge the fact that, hey—it didn't work out, but we can still be friends, right?

SENDING HIM RUNNING

Unfortunately, there are more things you can do wrong than right in the initial stages of a relationship. The committable faux pas are so numerous that to list them all would be truly intimidating. Instead I'll just list 10 major ones. Believe me, you will never see your millionaire again if you do any of the following:

1. Insist that your children come along on the first date.
2. Ask him to help you out with your "financial difficulties."
3. Ask him, on the third date, what colors he favors for the wedding.
4. Make a habit of loudly burping or making other gross body noises.
5. As you drive home, ask him if he'll swing you by the prison to visit your father who is doing time for embezzlement.
6. Chew tobacco.
7. Expect him to empty your garbage which hasn't been taken out in three weeks.
8. Wear marabou to bed.
9. Fight with his mother.

10. Inquire about the beneficiary of his life insurance policy.

Believe it or not, I know women who have committed all the heinous mistakes mentioned above. Just use common sense.

How To Keep the Home Fires Burning

So what exactly *should* you do to keep your wealthy man coming back for more? I asked a number of millionaires what makes them happy in a relationship, and this is what they told me:

"I love it when the woman I'm dating smiles and looks at me when I walk into the room," says Darby, a talented artist. "It's just a little thing, but it makes me feel warm and loved. So many women try to feign indifference."

"Home cooking!" says Don enthusiastically. He's a Texan, and involved in, what else? Oil. "I can eat in a fine restaurant every day of my life, but it's just not the same as it is when someone prepares something especially for me. I know it's a lot of work, and I appreciate that. I also like the intimacy and romance of eating alone together, rather than being in the midst of a hundred people, anyone of whom might come up to shake my hand at any second. Show me a woman who will cook for me at home, and I'll be her love slave forever!"

"I like it when a woman has other interests outside of me and mine," says Rob, a business executive from a very wealthy family. "She's too much of a burden if her world revolves around me. It's all I can do to keep myself spinning. I like to get support from her every now and then, rather than having to give her support all the time."

"Enthusiasm! Energy! But the positive kind, not the nervous kind," says Andre, a professional athlete. "I don't like a woman who mopes and whines all the time. I like it when she charges me up, not brings me down."

"What I'm looking for is a woman I can implicitly trust," says Evan, a prominent attorney. "I'm so tired of women who I can tell are constantly searching for someone better. I'd like to feel as if she won't look at another man while she's seeing me, as if I can completely satisfy her."

"Legs! I can overlook a big butt and a flat chest if the girl's got great, wild legs," says Spink, a rock musician who is nouveau riche. I came close to deleting his opinion.

"If a woman can learn to love and get along with my family and friends as well as I do, she might be the one for me," says Per, an entrepreneur. "I've known my family and friends a lot longer than I've known her, and I trust their judgment. I think they're great people, and I get along with them fine. There's no reason why she shouldn't be able to, although I guess some women feel they're in competition."

"I've got to have a woman who trusts me, who gives me my freedom knowing that I won't abuse it," says Tad, a media personality. "If she has to watch my every step and accuses me of fooling around all the time, I'm more tempted to do it."

"I like a woman who's just as comfortable on my Harley or in my bed as she would be at a state dinner," says Mike, in a rather frank moment. "I like a woman who is like a chameleon, and can adapt to any mood, any situation."

"A woman who will support and encourage me in my interests and my efforts," says Antonio, a stately older gentlemen whom I'd love to introduce to my mother. "It touches me when a woman makes the effort to take an interest in what I'm doing, and adds that to her own personal pursuits."

"Healthy and energetic. Those two qualities turn

me on," says Damian, a true promoter. "I can't stand it when a woman uses her poor health as an excuse to get me to feel sorry for her, to get me to want to take care of her. I want her to love life. Everybody gets sick every now and then, and that's okay. I just don't want a mopey hypochondriac."

"I know a wench of excellent discourse," says Balthazar, a wealthy merchant in Shakespeare's *The Comedy of Errors*. "Pretty and witty; wild, and yet, too, gentle;"

Those are some rather interesting insights, wouldn't you agree? It would be virtually impossible if you tried to be all those things all those men asked for, but the good news is, you don't have to be. The trick is to discern what your current man needs, and then decide whether or not you feel like giving it. At the same time, you mustn't overlook your own satisfaction. Is he equipped to fill *your* needs? If you decide he is and you want to pursue the relationship, let's borrow some ideas from these men, and see how you can utilize them to your benefit.

A Very Very Very Fine House

When your millionaire invites you to his place of residence, you'll be doing a lot of evaluating. His environment can tell you quite a bit about him. Scrutinize his living space closely. But realize that *your* environment will tell him a lot about you as well, and that his evaluation process will be every bit as exacting as yours. He will also probably have the chance to view your living space before you view his, since he definitely should offer to pick you up the first time you go out. Under rare circumstances, he'll send a car for you. But in most cases, be prepared to have him see where you live, and make him as comfortable as possible. You want him to return, don't you?

Your place does not have to be a perfectly appointed penthouse or a country estate. It does have to be clean and uncluttered however. Your ability to organize a home will leave an impression on him. My friend Sheila, the one we're trying to "culturize," once said, "Yeah, but if he's really rich, when I marry him we could have lots of maids and stuff to take care of the house. It doesn't really matter if *I* know how to do housework, does it?"

It doesn't matter *who* does the housework. What's important is that he sees that you value neatness, and know how to maintain it. A trashy residence might indicate a trashy demeanor, in the millionaire's mind. My condo is almost always immaculate. I force myself to do the housework thing at least once a week, and I see that clutter doesn't get out of hand in-between. The one exception is my desk, which is constantly strewn with envelopes, papers, computer paraphernalia, and various other debris. "I can't be *creative* in an area that's too structured," I tell them, and they usually forgive me that. An artist's studio wouldn't have to be perfectly arranged and neat either.

There are certain things that you can have in your home that will make you both more comfortable when he's visiting. They're not all expensive, and they're not all essential, but see what you can do to acquire the following:

> *Art prints, neatly hung*
> *Original art, if you can afford something good. Aunt Mary's cubist pastorals do not show off your taste at its best.*
> *Upscale, well-written publications like* The Wall Street Journal, Metropolitan Home, Vanity Fair, Modern Architecture, *your local city's magazine (he might be mentioned in it),* Sports Illustrated, The New Yorker, *a daily paper, a weekly news magazine, etc.*
> *Lit candles (very romantic)*
> *An espresso machine*

Decent books (he will go to your bookcase and try to discern what kind of person you are from the books you read. This is a quick way to impress or depress him. He will know, however, if the books are there for show, or if you really read them)

Fresh flowers

Fresh-smelling potpourri if the flowers and candles don't do the trick

Good music

An inviting couch

Cable TV, but not blaring when he walks in

Well-tended plants

Big, fluffy towels

Interesting sculptures or tasteful curios that have some significance. I usually try to pick up one representative, interesting, and artful piece from each country I visit. Among them are an Israeli menorah, a Guatemalan huipil, Egyptian funeral urns, Chinese enamel, and Puerto Rican butterflies. They're all conversation starters.

A telephone answering machine—but never play your messages in front of him. An ignored blinking message light will make you appear popular, and drive him mad with curiosity.

A large, comfortable looking bed

*A computer—this isn't essential, but it does convey
the idea that you're high tech, organized, and
intelligent.*

Fresh-smelling, clean soap in the bathrooms

By the same token, there are a few items that you
want to avoid displaying when your millionaire is
around. They will make you both uncomfortable.
They include:

*Beefcake or hard rock posters thumbtacked to the
wall*

*Velvet paintings of Elvis, voluptuous young women,
or unicorns*

*Periodicals like, The Star, The National Enquirer,
or Tiger Beat*

Fuzzy toilet seat covers

*Crocheted toilet-paper cozies sitting in your bathroom,
á la dolls with big skirts, pink poodles, or pandas*

Dead bug carcasses

Harlequin romances in your bookcase

Crossword puzzle books in your bathroom

*Pet hair—especially on dark furniture where it
looks like it's ready to jump on his suit*

Obnoxious pets

Obnoxious children

Bad odors like stale cigarette smoke and old garbage

Dirty dishes

Dead plants

Pictures of your ex

Lots of dust-covered, dried flowers

Frail furniture that looks as if it would break or stain if used

Moldy growth in the refrigerator

Matted shag carpet

An abundance of medication sitting around

An unmade bed

Ninja Turtle sheets

Grimy bathrooms

Dirty laundry

A zoo of stuffed animals

I can assure you that, if he walks into your home and feels pleased and relaxed, he'll be back, again and again. But let's put the shoe on the other foot. If you walk into his house and he has an excess of the following, make sure you leave soon and never come back. These are definite danger signals:

An excess of pornographic material. A Playboy or two is probably common, but hard-core books, magazines, and videos are frightening.

A telescope, pointed at the neighbors' window rather than at the stars.

An outrageous mess. He should care enough to clean things up before you come over.

Walls plastered with photos of him, especially big, moody headshots. Also, a myriad of mirrors on almost every wall. Even if he models, this is an indication that he's far too self-possessed.

Many pictures of him with his ex-wife. This is a sign he hasn't gotten over her yet.

An abundance of sexual paraphernalia left out on display. This will tell you that he's more interested in sexual adventures than in the relationship that should go with them.

Other women's belongings. If he cares about seeing you again, he will put these things away before you arrive.

Drug accouterments. You don't want to get involved with someone using non prescription drugs, not even steroids. These men will be unpredictable and unstable, plus they could get you in trouble with the law.

So, if your place passes his inspection, and his place passes your inspection, and you decide you want to see him again, allow me to give you a tip that will assure you his company again and again.

THE WAY TO A MAN'S HEART

Two words: *Feed him!* Most wealthy men will do absolutely anything for a homecooked meal. It's likely the majority of their meals are eaten in expensive restaurants, or over-prepared by indifferent servants. What they wouldn't give for a meal like mom, or their loving cook, used to make.

If your man treats you to elegant meals in fine restaurants, the least you can do is reciprocate by inviting him in for a meal at your house. You owe it to him. Besides, eating at home rather than in a restaurant is much less expensive for you, and your place is a far more intimate setting. This can lead to a better dessert than anything you could order in the best restaurant.

Many busy women today don't have time to bother with preparing a meal, and therefore never learn how. As busy as I am, I *love* to take the time to cook for someone I enjoy. To me, it's a creative process, and the outcome has the unique ability to please all five senses. Hopefully it sounds wonderful as I describe it. It smells fantastic as I cook it, it looks magnificent when I serve it, and it even feels sumptuous as we eat it. If you can, look at it as a challenge to create such a sensual masterpiece. You can do it.

Anyone who knows how to read a recipe is capable.

For your money, probably the best investment you can make in your culinary skills is to take a cooking class and buy a very reliable cookbook. The second best investment you can make is in a bread baking machine.

Is there a soul on earth who doesn't salivate when they smell the wonderful aroma of hot bread? Your millionaire will be smitten the second he walks in the door if that's the first thing that accosts his senses. It takes me no more than ten minutes of effort to throw together a loaf of steamy bread, but I get at least ten days' worth of mileage out of it. The men remember—especially if I give them a loaf to take home with them. I've had men confess that they'll sometimes wander by my door with the hope of sniffing that enticing smell, and that's not an easy thing to do, since I live in a tight security building. I always wondered how some manage to stop by just as I'm taking the bread out of the oven. Perhaps they're in collusion with the security guards.

Another nice culinary gadget to have around the house is, at best an espresso machine, but at least a coffee maker. There are so many fun, flavored coffees out these days, and a steaming cup of it will invite him to linger longer. I personally can't drink caffeine, so I make decaf, and with flavors like amaretto or Kahlua fudge, very few people can tell the difference. I cannot begin to tell you, though, how many intimate conversations I've had over a fine, warm, brew.

Like impressive coffee, impressive cooking is not that difficult these days. Of course it's not easy to master the techniques of gourmet chefs, but remember, your millionaire tastes the wares of gourmet chefs almost daily. He may be tired of that, and just want something he usually can't get in a restaurant. Don't be intimidated. Learn how to make at least three really scrumptious dishes. It won't kill you. Practice them a time or two with your girlfriends or family before you serve them to the man you're trying to impress, however. You don't want him to feel like an experiment, or to doubt your culinary skills.

He won't hate you if you don't know how to cook, but for some reason, men are always impressed by women who know how to prepare a good meal. Millionaires seem to trust them more. Perhaps it reminds some of them of their mothers.

When I cook, I like to start from scratch if I can, but when I'm in a hurry, that's not always an option. I'm not above using a can, jar, or box, but I always hide them deep down in the garbage so my wealthy friend believes I've been slaving for him all day.

Just to show you how easy, yet how impressive this can be, I'm going to share with you some of my favorite recipes and menus. These meals have never achieved anything less than the highest kudos. I use a number of shortcuts here, but don't turn your nose up if you're a purist. I've never heard a complaint yet. I'll give you advice for each; breakfast, lunch and dinner.

Dynamic Dinner

This centers around a very exotic dish that's more labor intensive than complicated. It's unusual enough so that your millionaire probably won't be disappointed if it isn't exactly like Mom used to make. As a matter of fact, most moms, unless they're from Spain or Cuba, never used to make this dish at all. It's called Paella (Paw-aye-ya), and it contains one of the most expensive (don't worry, you only use a pinch) spices in the world: saffron. I learned this version while sitting in the kitchen of a lively, middle-aged Andalucian woman who had been making it since she was seven. Now it's being passed on to you.

PAELLA

1-1/2 cups rice

1/2 lb. small scallops

1/2 lb. shrimp (in shells)

4 chicken drumsticks

3 cups boiling water

3 Tbsp. olive oil

1 small tomato, diced

1 lemon

3 cloves garlic (minced)

1/2 cup peas

1/2 cup pimento-stuffed olives

1 small diced onion

1/4 tsp. saffron

1 green bell pepper

1 red bell pepper

1 small jar artichoke hearts

Pour olive oil in large frying pan and heat on medium. Sauté garlic, onions, and drumsticks in oil, until onions are transparent, about five minutes. Add rice. Stir a few minutes, until rice becomes slightly opaque. Add water and saffron to mixture, in that order, and simmer. While it's simmering, chop peppers, half into half-inch squares, half into long slices, (about 1/4 inch wide), the length of the pepper. Add pepper squares, tomato, and washed scallops; stir. Simmer about 10 minutes more, stirring occasionally. While simmering, wash shrimp but do not remove legs or shells. Add frozen peas, artichoke hearts, and olives to rice and stir well, then arrange the raw shrimp in an artistic pattern on top of the simmering mixture. Push them down slightly, so they cook. Let them cook 5 minutes on one side, then turn them over and let them cook five minutes on the other. Arrange remaining pepper slices on top, in a pinwheel pattern, alternating red and green. Let simmer 5 minutes more, or until rice is tender. You may have to add a little more water so the rice can cook a little longer.

While you're waiting for the dish to finish, slice the lemon. Take some lemon juice and rub it on your fingers. By now they've picked up a strong odor of garlic and onions, and you don't want your hands smelling like that later. The lemon juice should fix it. Take the remaining lemon slices and arrange them around the side of the pan. Many people like to squeeze the juice on their paella.

Bring the dish to the table with a flourish, so your man can see your masterpiece and be sufficiently impressed. It should be a work of art, with the yellow rice, pink shrimp, and red and green peppers. Many of the men to whom I've served Paella have wanted to photograph it.

You can add to the table some crusty white European bread and a cucumber, tomato salad with vinaigrette dressing and basil, and you've got one incredible meal.

If you really want to impress him, for dessert, try a flan. Those of you who have attempted it before will roll your eyes skyward, but I've found a wonderful shortcut that comes out better than most made from scratch.

First take one cup of sugar, and melt it on the stove, over medium heat, stirring constantly. Once it turns into a beautiful golden-brown liquid, pour it immediately into a mixing bowl (not plastic) and turn it so the sides are completely coated. Be careful. Caramelized sugar can burn you. Set the bowl aside. Next take two boxes of Jell-O-Americana Custard, and follow the directions on the box, omitting one-half a cup of milk. (one quarter cup for each box). As the custard is cooking, add at least one tablespoon of brandy or rum. When the custard is done, pour it into the caramel-coated bowl, and put the whole concoction in the fridge for at least three hours. Just before serving, invert the bowl on a plate that has slightly raised sides (to catch the caramel sauce.) You'll be amazed at how easily it slides right out of the bowl. Cut it in slices, and spoon on the extra caramel sauce when you serve it.

LUSCIOUS LUNCH

If your millionaire is coming by for lunch, I'd suggest something hardy, yet elegant like Chicken

Tortellini Soup. To give credit where it's due, I got this recipe from my sister. (She didn't marry a millionaire, but she and her husband are now close.) You'll want to whip up a loaf of bread in your machine to go along with it, and I usually serve my homemade strawberry freezer jam to go on top of that. If you didn't do jam last spring, honey and butter will do.

CHICKEN TORTELLINI SOUP

9 oz. broccoli	2 onions, diced
3 cans chicken broth	4 cups water
3 cans cream of	1 cup sliced carrots
chicken soup	1/2 tsp. garlic powder
6 chicken breasts, cooked	1/2 tsp. nutmeg
and shredded	1/2 tsp. oregano
1-7 oz. package of	1/2 tsp. basil
cheese tortellini	

Mix everything in a large pot except tortellini and broccoli. Bring to a boil, then let simmer for half an hour. Add broccoli and tortellini and let simmer ten minutes more. Voila! It's ready! Wasn't that easy?

If you want to have a fun, lunchtime dessert on hand, try applesauce chocolate chip cookies. Actually, they're useful to have around anytime in case someone drops by, and I can assure you that your millionaire will not be able to pick these up at Mrs. Field's in the local mall.

APPLESAUCE
CHOCOLATE CHIP COOKIES

1 cup sugar	1 tsp. salt
1/2 cup shortening	1 large pkg. chocolate chips
1 cup applesauce	2-1/2 cups flour
1 tsp. cinnamon	2 eggs
1 tsp. nutmeg	1 tsp. baking soda

Mix applesauce and baking soda in a large bowl and set aside. In a separate bowl, cream together sugar, shortening, and eggs, then add that mixture to the sauce. Add flour, sifting it with spices. Last, add the chocolate chips. Drop heaping tablespoons full on a greased cookie sheets, and bake for 12 minutes at 350. Makes about 3 dozen cookies.

BREATHTAKING BREAKFAST

The main course for this breakfast is another Spanish dish that I've Americanized. I learned much more than a second language in the years I spent abroad. In Spain they'll usually eat it for lunch or dinner, but because it has eggs and potatoes in it, most American men prefer it in the morning. This menu will also work well for a breakfast picnic. How excited your millionaire would be if you had the creativity to spoil him with a sunrise repast! He'll still be impressed, however, if this is served to him in the privacy of your own home.

TORTILLA ESPAÑOLA

2 cups potatoes, peeled, cubed, and fried in olive oil

or

1/2 package of Inland Valley Tater Babies (or any other large cube-type frozen potato), heated in the oven as directed on the package. (This is 100% easier, and 75% less to clean up.)

5 eggs

2 Tbsp. dried onion flakes

salt, to taste

1 Tbsp. olive oil

While potatoes are in oven, break five eggs in a bowl and beat them. Add onion flakes, and several shakes of salt. When potatoes are done, cut them into bite-sized pieces, and add them to egg mixture, making sure they're all coated. Pour the mixture into small, round-edged, non-stick frying pan (like an omelet pan) with heated olive oil in it. Cook on low-medium until the egg has set, and the edges, when lifted from the pan with a spatula, are light golden brown, about five minutes. Here comes the slightly tricky part. Remove pan from heat, and place a large plate, face down, over the mixture. Rapidly flip it over onto the plate, without breaking the tortilla. Then slide the tortilla back into the pan to cook the other side. Use the spatula to tuck the edges back under, if necessary. Continue cooking on low heat, for about five minutes more, until the other side is the same golden brown as the top. Be careful not to burn. When done, slide tortilla out of pan and onto another plate, with the best-looking side facing up. It should look sort of like a delicious, golden-brown torte with rounded edges. Serve it in wedges alone, with salsa, or, if you must, ketchup.

Fruit, fresh-squeezed juice, and some bran muffins make this meal complete. After that, you certainly won't be hungry for lunch. The tortilla, by the way, stores well in the fridge. I've had men come 'round specifically asking if I have any tortilla leftovers.

So there you have it. Menus for any hour of the day or night. Use them as much as you like, or try to find your own unusual recipes that you can master and throw together at a moment's notice. Spending time in the kitchen isn't so bad after all now, is it?

Especially when you consider the mileage you get from it.

I must warn you however, that inviting a millionaire over for an intimate meal could lead the relationship onto some rather volatile ground, if it hasn't been there already. Let's see if we can figure out how to deal with that.

SEX

There are some women who think the way to a man's heart is through his fly. Wrong! As a matter of fact, I'd like to suggest just the opposite. Sleep with him too soon, and you'll never get any nearer to his heart than his pelvis. Make an end run around the genitals, and you just might score the winning touchdown, if that's what you're looking for. I'll give you two rather intense examples to illustrate this, and I'm sure there are billions more.

Lana had wildly wealthy Lance in her pocket. Although she considered him no more than a close friend, he was mad about her, and didn't fail to show it. Lana saw other people, but Lance was obsessed only with Lana. When they were together, he was constantly cajoling her to sleep with him. He would often leave very expensive gifts on her doorstep. He was always finding little things to fix around her house. He sent all sorts of lucrative business her way. He filled her office with flowers on a weekly basis. He invited her on long, luxurious trips, offering to pick up all the expenses. The only catch was that she would have to stay in his room, "wink, wink."

Lana truly felt affection for this very generous man, but she saw no reason to sleep with him. Oh, there was a little chemistry there, but she just didn't want a relationship with him on that level. Until one night.

Lana's other relationships had turned sour, and she was feeling rather depressed. "Why not Lance?" she began wondering. "He certainly is thoughtful, unlike these other dogs I've been seeing, and he does take good care of me. Perhaps it's time to take our relationship a little farther."

She planned the evening carefully, telling him she wanted to have him over for dinner to thank him for all the wonderful things he'd done. He was in heaven. Afterward, as they cuddled on the couch and got to the point where he usually tried to score and she usually called foul, she took his hand and led him toward the bedroom. Lance couldn't believe his luck. He had his clothes off before he left the living room. They barely made it to the bed, and the passion was intense. So intense, that Lana experienced a change of heart. Why had she put Lance off all these months? This was incredible! Perhaps she'd finally found her own true love.

You can imagine how surprised she was when, 20 minutes later, Lance started hurriedly collecting his clothes and muttering something about an "early appointment tomorrow morning." She had hoped to spend the entire night in his arms. He'd certainly talked about it enough. "Call me!" she said, as he hurried out the door, forgetting that those are words desperate women cry as a last resort. Fears that the call will never come are almost always correct.

Lana's were. She didn't hear from Lance for over a month, and when she finally did, it was Lana who made the call. "I've, uh, been busy, and I had to go out of town," he stammered. She later found out that he'd 'had' to go to Hawaii with a 21-year-old member of his staff who stayed in his room, "wink, wink." He was history for Lana, obviously more intent on the conquest than on savoring the spoils. Lana was left feeling lonely, empty, and foolish.

If only she'd listened to the stories we'd both heard as we were growing up—you know the ones I'm talking about. You've heard them too. They talk about people wanting what they can't have, and about not having to buy the cow if you can get the milk for free. They're rather sad but true. I've decided to heed them, and they've never failed me yet.

I can think of one instance in particular. Richard was giving me the Lance rush, and I enjoyed it, but I had no intention of actually going to bed with him. I told him so, in a very nice way, of course. "I guess you could say I'm just old-fashioned in that respect. It's not that I don't find you attractive. As a matter of fact, you're one of the most scintillating men I've ever met, and it's with great effort that I refrain myself from dragging you into the bedroom and having my way with you right this very moment!" (they love hearing that sort of thing). "It's just that I don't believe our relationship is at a level where I think it's appropriate. And I don't think it ever will be until we're truly committed to each other."

"I'll never commit to a woman who I can't sleep with first," he said in frustration. "How would we know if we're sexually compatible? How would we ever build any intimacy in the relationship? That's the one thing I have to find out before I get married. Nope. I'll *never* marry a woman without knowing what she's like in bed."

Three weeks later I got a phone call from Richard, in the middle of the night. "L.A." he said in an anguished tone. "I can't stand this any longer. I'm lying here thinking of you, and it's driving me mad. Let's put aside our differences, and go get married *as soon as possible*. I love you. I have to have you. I promise to be everything you ever wanted or needed. *Please!*"

There are occasions, like when I'm struggling to cover expenses at the end of the month, that I think perhaps I should have taken Richard up on his offer. He was serious, you know, and he would have gone through with it. But I wasn't ready for marriage with him. I didn't love him enough, and I never was able to. The vast majority of the time, I don't regret turning him down. And after listening to Lana's horror story and others like it, I don't regret not sleeping with him. I feel I would have been like so many others if I had. As it was, I was the one who stood out. The one he wanted to marry.

The fact is, these days, it's not only unwise, but deathly dangerous to sleep with the men you date, whether they have mountains of money or not. Sexually transmitted diseases are rampant among all classes, and they can ruin your life. AIDS, of course, can kill you, but other types of common STDs can also wreck havoc. Charlotte has a mild case of herpes, which hardly affects her physically. Still, she must explain that to every man she gets close to, and many of them run for their lives. Although she has money and power, she cannot buy their health back for them once they are infected, and they realize this.

Many people believe that the condom is the panacea for prevention of all STDs. Condoms can indeed reduce the risk, but they cannot guarantee complete safety. As cliché as it may sound, having sex even with a condom, with someone whose health is uncertain, is as dangerous as playing Russian roulette. Besides, when it comes right down to it, most men will tell you they detest wearing condoms. Some even have problems maintaining an erection with condoms on, and will try to convince you to let them go unsheathed. Don't you dare fall for that! If you ever sleep with a millionaire, you want it to be as great an experience as it can possibly be, without fear or inhibition. Unfortunately, the health situation today and the necessity for condoms precludes that. It's better to wait until you are absolutely certain.

By the way, HIV positivity can take up to six months to show up on a test. Actually, the only way to be certain that you or your partner are not HIV positive is to be tested six months after your last sexual experience, and then have relations only with those who have also waited at least six months and then been tested. Good luck finding two people who have been sexually active and meet those criteria.

"But what if I'm certain he's clean, and we really want to sleep with each other?" you might ask. "There are plenty of other women who will do anything for him. Won't he drop me for them?" Sure there are plenty of other women who will do anything for him. What there aren't are plenty of women who won't. Millionaires' lives are full of women who would sleep with them in a New York minute, believing they can get to his heart or his wallet through his loins. They're wrong. They might do in a pinch, but what he wants in the long run is someone he can trust, someone who is unfailingly clean, someone to whom he is a special, precious, *rare*, commodity. I can honestly say I have never lost a man I cared about to a woman who *would* sleep with him when I wouldn't.

By not sleeping with him, you become an enigma, a puzzle, a challenge, and there is nothing a millionaire likes more than a challenge. The millionaire covets the prize no other man can acquire, the treasure he alone, with his unique, individual talents can win.

Of course, you need to convince him that you

are a treasure worth having. As a matter of fact, you need to convince him that you are the hottest little treasure on earth. And you are, aren't you? You are a seething, passionate human being. You have to let him know that.

Playfully share your fantasies with him. Tell him what you're absolutely dying to do to him...someday. Let your body confirm that. When you're kissing and embracing and the heat is rising, don't try to control your breath—let it come out fast and heavy. Let those soft, passionate moans rise from the back of your throat. Let your hips move freely, gyrating and pressing against his. Give your hands license to wander and caress. Erase all doubt from his mind that there could ever be a degree of frigidity in you. Show him that your combined passion could be the most incendiary, combustible power on earth. But don't consummate it.

If you think he will be grateful to you because you have intercourse with him, and he will therefore take better care of you, you're wrong. In a way, you're selling your body for the gifts and favors you want from him, not unlike a prostitute, and he will realize that. The last thing he wants to spend large amounts of time with is a whore. If you think the path to the chapel goes through the bedroom, or that with sex you can entice him or make him feel obligated to marry you, you're wrong again. I can assure you, he's gotten around that many times before.

But what about your own needs, you might ask. As a passionate human being, it isn't *natural* to resist those very basic desires. Well, you've got a point there. And when I see a large diamond necklace in a jewelry store, my natural, basic desire is to reach out, grab it, and wear it home, but I have to discipline myself and resist those urges, or suffer the consequences. If I'm willing to wait, to earn the money for it, and then, when the time is right, come back and pick it up legally and legitimately, it can be mine forever, and I can wear it with pride. Do you get my point?

Now, there are many women happily married to millionaires who point out that *they* had perfectly satisfying sex lives with their husbands before they tied the knot, and look where it got *them*. That may be so, and I am happy that their marriages are successful. But I'd also like to draw their attention to the fact that there are far more women who had perfectly satisfying sex lives with their millionaires and never made it to the alter. I've never spoken with a woman who regretted *not* having slept with a millionaire. But I've spoken to plenty who regret having slept with one. You just have to decide which camp you prefer.

If you're truly interested in marrying the millionaire you're dating, I would suggest that you put off sleeping with him until you're both committed. If you're just looking for a good time with him, I would suggest you do whatever you must keep yourself free of any kind of physical or emotional risk.

I'm the first to admit that it's tough to hold back. But if you play your cards right, you won't have to hold back for long. It shouldn't take many months to convince him that you are a scintillating, trustworthy asset that he can no longer live without. Some women can do that in an evening. I'd advise you to spend at least six months or more seeing him before you make that ultimate commitment. The next section gives you some ways to accomplish that.

BECOMING A SOUL MATE

When it comes right down to it, satisfying your millionaire's stomach and loins are skills that can be acquired with some effort. It's satisfying his soul that takes tremendous insight, sensitivity, and work. How does one satisfy anyone's soul? Here is a list of ideas that men of wealth have told me would definitely fulfill them.

Don't compare him to others. Deep down inside, the millionaire would like to feel as if he's the only one you ever truly loved. He wants to be accepted or rejected for his own qualities, and not the ones you attribute to him because you've "dated men like him before." (Incidentally, he'd also like to feel as if he's the only one you've ever truly enjoyed making love to. Wouldn't we all?)

Show appreciation. Although millionaires often give more, many times they're shown less appreciation. "Pearls? I guess they're all right, but I really wanted diamonds." Remember, he doesn't have to give you anything. Be grateful for whatever good things he sends your way.

Reciprocate! Some women feel that since he has all the money, he should do all the giving. Not so! He is human, and enjoys receiving gifts just as much as you do. Since he usually buys himself any expensive item he wants, however, gift giving is considerably more difficult for you. He will understand this, and realize it's the thought that counts. My solution to this problem is to give hand-made gifts or wittily written letters or poetry. For several Christmases now I've made the wealthy men in my life elegant forest green velvet Christmas stockings, with their names embroidered in Old English letters across the top. I fill these one-of-a-kind items with their favorite trinkets—aftershave, candy, silk boxers, books, CDs, etc. One man got tears in his eyes as he opened it, telling me he'd never received a handmade gift before. Another year, I got some girlfriends together and had an old-fashioned quilting bee. The outcome was a beautiful, paisley quilt that the recipient, who can easily acquire far more luxurious linens, still considers one of his most prized possessions.

Give him the benefit of the doubt. Once you've decided you can trust him, don't always jump to the worst conclusions. Believe him when he tells you he's working late, that his relationship with his ex-wife is purely pla-tonic, that he's acting honorably when he's out of town. Your mistrust can frustrate him and encourage him to live up (or down) to your expectations. If you've checked him out and he appears to have integrity, don't doubt him.

Be trustworthy. Don't go out of your way to make him jealous. This is game playing, and many millionaires simply do not have time for it. If he thinks he can depend on you to be on time, to keep from embarrassing him, to be faithful to him, to love him, do not let him down. Trust can be hard, if not impossible, to rebuild.

Show an interest in his work. For many millionaires, their work is their life, especially if they're self-made. They will spend long hours and lots of energy building their own empire, and many times they'll want to share their enthusiasm with you. They will know if you are vacantly nodding your head and pretending to listen. Find out as much as you can about what they do, and apply that knowledge when conversing with them.

Do not be possessive. He is not your property, nor are you his. Do not get in the habit of demanding anything from him, or of resenting anything else that requires his time and attention. Wouldn't you be upset if he wanted to know every little thing you did at every minute of the day, and became extremely jealous when you so much as looked at another man, let alone talked to him? Just as you need your space, he needs his. Give it to him.

Don't expect too much too soon. The millionaire will feel the pressure you're putting on him, and buck. This is a habit many of us get into. After three dates and some very intimate moments, we expect them to be completely devoted to us and our relationship. When I was quite a bit younger, I remember seeing a wealthy man I'd been dating for two weeks, at the opera, with another woman. I was with another man, of course, but he was just a friend. I had no idea who this wench was that 'my' millionaire was escorting. I seethed, and when he called me later, I was less than civil. Without my having to mention it, he knew exactly what had incurred my wrath, and he was not impressed. My being unreasonable clearly put a damper on our relationship.

Help him relax. Millionaires are often so wrapped up in their business projects that it can take a considerable amount of massaging and soft music, or perhaps a good, vigorous game of tennis, to get them to wind down. Find out what he needs, when he needs it, and provide it for him. This is not demeaning. This is assisting another human being, and helping to make his life less stressful.

Love him. That deep, tender feeling that only a woman in love can radiate, will make him feel that he is the richest man in the world, no matter what his financial status. If he is ready for it, open to it, and expresses that he feels the same way, don't hold back to gain control of him, or of your own feelings. Let the emotion poor forth. It will feel wonderful for both of you. And if the relationship doesn't end the way you would like it to, at least you'll be able to say that you gave it your best shot.

You cannot control the way another person acts, but you certainly can control yourself. If your relationship with your millionaire is not going the way you'd like it to, see if you're following the ten suggestions listed previously, and try to adjust.

If you're doing all you possibly can and the relationship is still not working, try discussing your doubts with him. If he seems indifferent about it all, you might consider turning him loose and casting your line back in the water. After all, once you've hooked one millionaire, the next one will be much easier, and the one after that easier still. You will have a reputation for dating wealthy men, and others will seek you out. The following chapter will help you deal with that.

SAYING GOODBYE GRACEFULLY

"I can't believe you and Clinton are back together!" Jean exclaimed after she'd seen us one night at a movie screening. "I thought your romance was ancient history!"

"It is, but we still do things together," I told her. "He knows I love to see art films."

"I don't know how you do that," she said, shaking her head. "When I break up with a man, he usually runs screaming into the night and I never see him again. But you seem to turn them into friends. How does that work?"

I think, if I've been blessed with any gifts at all,

one is the ability to make a smooth transition from "lovers" to friends. I believe it's a great shame to lose contact with someone you were once very close to, who you've shared so much with, who knows you so well. I do all I can to see that, even when the fireworks die, there is still a warm glow that we both appreciate.

Of course, it is much easier if I am the one who is leaving and he is the one who is left. If he leaves me in a particularly unceremonious fashion, my first inclinations are to ruin his business deals, key his expensive car, drive my car through his petunia patch, and to boil his bunny. I allow myself about an hour to fantasize about revenge, and then I try to put it out of my mind. In all honesty, I don't want to be a candidate for an appearance on Donahue when they're featuring "Convicts with fatal attractions." I try to tell myself that success is the best revenge of all, and I try to focus on achieving it.

Besides, the millionaire community can be rather tight, and if I go crazy on one, others will soon hear about it, and I will ruin my own further chances. What I really want is the affirmation that even without this man in my life, I am still an attractive and valid person. One way to prove that to myself is by turning the heartbreaker into a platonic friend.

I've found the best way to do this is to be up front about it. I have a speech all prepared for these incidents. "I understand this isn't working for you romantically," I'll say. "I'm sorry about that, but I guess those are the breaks. I still think you're a wonderful person, however, and I hope you feel the same way about me. I hope you will still feel free to call me if you ever need anything, or if you just want to talk. I also hope you'd feel good about introducing me to any interesting friends you might have who you feel would be more my type. In the meantime, Jesse Trowbridge has always thought very highly of you, and if you'd like, I can give you her number. I wish nothing but the best for you."

Mentioning dating other people indicates that you are well on your way to getting over him.

Of course this is easier said than done. Sometimes I'll need at least a week away from him before I can make that little altruistic speech. But I always try to make it, and mean it. It can do me nothing but good.

Let me give you an example. I became enamored of Clark not because he was wealthy, but because he was brilliant. Socially, however, he was an absolute derelict. He asked me to help him by teaching him social skills, and by introducing him to the right people. I took to my Pygmalion project with relish. I helped him dress, I helped him relax and converse at parties. I helped him acquire multitudes of friends. I also inadvertently helped him become more attractive to the woman he would eventually marry. I was deeply wounded when I realized what was happening. He was so socially maladroit that he didn't see how much I was hurting. He even took me out to dinner the night before he announced his engagement to the other woman. "L.A.," he said, "I've valued your opinion for so long, I want you to tell me if you think what I'm doing is right."

"Of course not, you idiot! You should be marrying me!" I wanted to scream. Instead I quietly asked him, "Clark, do you truly love her?"

"I do," he replied.

"Then go for it!" I told him.

Those were four of the most difficult words I ever said, but four of the most important. Once he was committed to someone else, all my hope with him was gone, and I could get him out of my system. I attended their wedding, their wedding brunch, their wedding reception. And through it all, I became close friends with his lively sister. She remains one of my dearest friends today, and I also stay close to Clark and his wife. All my romantic feelings for him are gone, and we all enjoy a very mutually satisfying relationship. I can't tell you how glad I am that I didn't boil his bunny.

As I said, if you are the one who is walking away, it makes everything infinitely easier. Your goal is to achieve the breakup with no hard feelings. Millionaire's egos can be exceptionally fragile here. They usually like calling the shots, and when someone takes that ability away from them, they're apt to revert to childishness. Chances are, when you oh-so-elegantly and adroitly give them the boot, you'll get responses like, "You ungrateful witch! After all I've done for you!" Or "You're a worthless moron for not realizing my value." Or "Excuse me? I didn't realize we had a relationship to terminate." Wealthy men generally have too much pride to beg and plead.

If you want to avoid all the negativism and keep it at a friendly level, the best thing to do is convince *him* that he's breaking up with *you*. "Donald," you could say, "you're so extraordinarily focused on your goals I just don't think I can ever satisfy you. I find myself far too distracted by other people and projects that I know I'd frustrate you down the road. So that I don't set myself up for devastating disappointment later on, do you think we could move to a more platonic relationship?" What you've just told him is that you think he's a selfish rogue and you'd prefer that he never touched you again. But he won't take it that way. He'll tell his friends, "I had to break up with Lola. She just couldn't handle my commitment to success. She's a nice kid, though."

Breaking up doesn't have to be so hard to do if you put maintaining everyone's respect at the top of your priority list. You want to be able to retain your self-respect, and at the same time retain a healthy respect for the man you're not seeing any more. You want him to retain his self-respect, and continue with a healthy respect for you. With that in mind, everyone wins.$

E I G H T

*Closing the Deal:
Are You Ready?*

Nuptials are nothing to trifle with. This is one of the biggest commitments you will ever make in your life. It's serious enough with the average guy, but millionaires come with their own special set of instructions that are unique and challenging. Before you lure your millionaire to the alter, you're going to have to prepare yourself. I'd suggest you ask yourself the following questions:

Am I prepared to look at this as a lifetime commitment, and not just something that, if it doesn't work out, can be fixed with a divorce?

You'll find that wealthy men take the institution of marriage more seriously than most, mainly because they have so much at stake financially. Even with prenuptial agreements, each divorce sends a millionaire reeling. If you are cavalier in your attitude about the duration of a marriage, the millionaire will discern this, and shy away.

How do I deal with the green-eyed monster?

There will be many opportunities for jealousy in your relationship, because there is a particularly vexing breed of amoral women out there who love the scent of money and will not let a wedding band deter them in their pursuit. Because your man is rich, many other women will be attracted to him. Will you be able to discipline yourself to ignore them and do you best with what you've got, or will you feel you have to question him every minute of every day, and about every word he exchanges with another woman? If you're inclined toward the latter, you'll probably make each other miserable.

Am I prepared to spend days, nights, and even weeks without him?

Even when you're married, you probably won't get the majority of your millionaire's time. Most men with mammoth amounts of money have monumental demands placed on them. You might feel as if you have to take a back seat to his work, or to other obligations. Can your ego take that? Do you have enough outside interests to keep you busy? Can you be supportive of him in his pursuits, even if they temporarily take him away from you?

Can I perform in public graciously, and on cue?

When you're the wife of a prominent man, you will be in the spotlight whether you want to be or not. People will expect you to set an example, and they will joyously jump upon your every faux pas. Think about it. Don't you particularly scrutinize the wives of the rich and famous? Can you endure the same scrutiny from others?

Am I financially responsible?

Don't believe that once you tie the knot, you will have *carte blanche* to run out and buy everything your heart desires. Even though you will probably have more money, you will still have to be responsible for it. If you constantly spend more than you have now, chances are you will do the same even when you have greater amounts of money. I would learn how to handle money well before I married a millionaire. If they've had their money for any length of time, they will be very responsible, and very disappointed in you if you're not.

Am I capable of adapting to the nuances of a more elite social set?

Once you marry a millionaire, your dinner parties will no longer be able to consist of a pot of spaghetti and red wine-in-a-box. If you've been running in a well-heeled crowd, you might have become accustomed to their tastes and habits, but there will still be some adjustments to make. Are you ready to make them?

Am I prepared for the conflict that will arise when my husband puts his job and interests first?

It's inevitable. Because your millionaire will make more money than you do, he will tend to trivialize your interests. Think about how you're going to handle that.

Can I cope with widespread envy?

There will be people who will begin treating you cruelly and callously, not for what you've done, but for what you have. Even your siblings could treat you differently. Is that something you're willing to deal with?

Can I "stand by my man?"

The wedding vows usually say "for better or for worse," and the problem with prominent men is that their 'worse' is often made quite public. If you're willing to partake of the fruits of his labors, can you handle a sour one every now and then, even when it's broadcast on the ten o'clock news?

If you can answer all these questions positively, congratulations! You're halfway there toward making an exceptional millionaire's wife. The next chapters will help you see what it takes to go the rest of the way.

A MOVE IN THE WRONG DIRECTION

You've been seeing an awful lot of each other lately. As a matter of fact, neither of you feels that all the time together in the world would be nearly be enough. You find it almost impossible to say goodbye when it's time to go home. The drive between your home and his seems unendurably long—a ridiculous waste of time. He asks you to move in. You pack your bags the next day, yes?

NO!

You might think that you're moving down the right road when he asks you to co-habitate, but stop and think about it for a minute. By asking you to move in with him, he is really asking you to give up one of your most valuable possessions, your freedom. And he's not offering you any security or commitment in return.

It may be extremely tempting, especially if his place is far more luxurious than yours (and the chances of that are pretty good). It may appear as though he's offering you an elegant lifestyle and unending companionship, but what he's really trying to do is make you one of his acquisitions, bought and paid for with a roof and meals. He really doesn't love you enough to share with you and give you legal title to all his possessions. He just wants you enough to count you among them.

And think of the position in which that places you! You have to take everything he dishes out because you're at his mercy for material comfort. If you were on your own and he began acting inappropriately, you could decide if you wanted to put up with it or not, and you would have the freedom to start searching for other options. But you can't start seeing other men while you're living under his roof.

"Oh, but what does a marriage certificate really mean? It's only a little piece of paper," many people say. My response is that a little piece of paper means quite a bit. It's a legal and tangible sign of commitment that does not exist where there's a live-in situation. I've discerned this by the number of men who approach me while they're living with someone else. "It's not working out," they confide in me. If there's no legal commitment, expelling a live-in can be a relatively simple and painless process.

Melanie would probably disagree with me. She's living with a wealthy, affable man I'll call Kyle. Melanie is not particularly interested in getting married or having children, but just wants decent, loyal companionship. She thinks she has the ideal situation with Kyle. He doesn't push her for a commitment, and she believes he is faithful and content with her. What she doesn't realize is that when Kyle is out of town, he plays quite the stallion.

I know this because he has a history of coming to see me. "What about your relationship with

Melanie?" I'll ask. "I don't want to get tangled up in a relationship that would hurt anyone."

"What she doesn't know won't hurt her," he replies. "She doesn't bring the same things into my life that you can."

That obviously doesn't sway me.

"Don't worry about it, L.A.," he goes on. "It's not like you'd be the only one to come between her and me. There have been others."

Can I tell you how attractive that made him sound? Here was a man saying, 'get involved with me. I do *unfaithful* often and well.' He was also indicating that he wasn't overly concerned about any contagious little 'presents' he might bring home to Melanie. When I pointed this out, he claimed neither I nor Melanie had anything to worry about, since he was always "very careful." Sure!

Actually, he believed a relationship with me, because I wouldn't sleep with him, wouldn't count as being disloyal to Melanie. I had to differ. He was trying to take me out to dinner, to seduce me, and he was sending me expensive presents. (I would have returned them if I knew where to send them without making Melanie suspicious.) Does that sound very loyal to you? I don't think Melanie would love it either. The very justification Kyle used for his actions was "Look. I'm not married to her! I'm just living with her!" Kyle is not the only man I've come across who acts this way.

If a millionaire wants the luxury of having a beautiful, attractive, intelligent woman in his home as his constant companion, let him pay the price for it. We don't come cheap. He needs to be just as committed to you as he is to that which made him rich. Chances are he's devoted his life to it. You're far more valuable. You deserve at least as much.

If you want to close that deal with him, there are some things that are non-negotiables. Your life is one of them. Don't let him have it until he's willing to pay your asking price.

ONE LAST CHECK

Let's take a breather here. You're considering one of the biggest moves you've ever made. You're thinking about actually devoting your life to another person. Are you absolutely positive that's what you want? Ask yourself this question: Is he worthy of you?

Just because he has money, he is not necessarily your perfect mate. Some wealthy men believe that money licenses them to treat people cruelly or thoughtlessly. You're too good to accept that.

When I met Amalia for lunch one day, she didn't take her sun glasses off as she entered the restaurant. I didn't notice immediately, because I was too busy admiring the ruby tennis bracelet her wealthy boyfriend had recently bestowed upon her. Finally I inquired about the shades, wondering if she had just been to the eye doctor and had her pupils dilated.

"No," she replied sheepishly. She slightly raised her glasses to reveal a huge purple and red swollen eye. "The bracelet was a peace offering." I was stunned. No gift or privilege, no matter how expensive, should be worth physical abuse. Amalia obviously didn't agree. To her, a black eye was a fair price to pay for expensive jewelry. Amalia has been involved in some truly tragic relationships, and it doesn't look as if they'll get better in the near future.

And then there's Ralph. "L.A.," he whined, "don't you have any beautiful friends you can introduce me to? I know about all those nasty date rape rumors that are circulating about me, but I figure my money can make up for that, can't it?"

Guess again, you dog. I wouldn't line you up with my garbage collector's pit bull. No one has to be subjected to that. It's not worth it for a good meal.

Among the things you should *never* put up with are:

Physical abuse—If he *ever* touches you with the intent to cause pain, run.

Verbal abuse—Never allow him to demean you in public or try to make you feel inferior or worthless in private.

Emotional abuse—You do not have to associate with someone who finds your sore spots, then sticks his finger in them and wiggles it around. If he is intentionally doing things that hurt you, leave him alone, no matter what his reasons.

Lying—Trust is an essential part of any relationship. If you cannot trust him, what the two of you have is not worth your valuable time or effort.

Selfish manipulation—If he tries to get you to compromise your own moral code for his own purposes, he does not respect you enough. And you definitely deserve respect.

There are just too many wonderful men out there to waste your time with a scoundrel just because he has money. And you certainly don't have to marry one. If you're convinced he will treat you well, and that you can love him forever, this is what you must do:

GOING IN FOR THE KILL

"The female of the species is more deadly than the male," according to Rudyard Kipling, and I'd have to agree when it comes to the human species. Most men believe their idea to get married came out of a vacuum, but we all know who really planted it there. At this point, if you haven't moved in with him and you haven't slept with him even though he's asked, you've probably got him right where you want him. Any one of the following dozen suggestions could be just what's needed to push him over the edge:

> *Make yourself indispensable to him.* This is first and foremost. Do things for him that he can't or doesn't like to do for himself, and point them out. Plant thoughts like "how did you ever survive without me?" in his head. Renee was a master of this. After they'd been dating for a while, Renee be-

came responsible for her millionaire's social schedule, reminding him of his appointments, and even dropping the appropriate clothes by his office if he didn't have them with him. "I had to marry her," he said. "It got so I would have been lost without her."

Make allies of his family and friends. If you can convince those around him that you are the best thing that ever walked into his life, they will help convince him. His children can be the most help of all, especially if they're young. By the way, some of the friends you make from your millionaire's circle will be around long after the man is gone. There are a multitude of great reasons for getting close to his friends and family.

Find out what his fears are, and assuage them. Does he worry that women only want him for his money? Convince him that you love him for what he is, not for what he has. Is he afraid of commitment? Show him that commitment to you could enhance his freedom in many ways. Does he doubt his ability to be a good father and husband? Let him know that he's the best you've ever hoped for, and that good parenting skills can be learned.

Convince him that you are a hot commodity. Every man wants what's attractive to other men. Let him know that you are. If other millionaires happen to be flirting with you, make sure he sees or casually finds out. Vince admits that he was encouraged to think lasting commitment when he saw notes by Valerie's phone every few days that said, "Call Dave." He also found a checklist of men's names among some notes by her bedside. His name wasn't on it, and it intrigued him. If a man called while he was at her house, she would smile into the phone and say, "Dirk, (or whoever), can I call you back later?" Even if it was the carpet cleaner, Vince didn't know that, and he began to wonder. Before long, he wanted her for himself.

Fill his life with things that remind him of you. Carry a camera often, and take pictures of the two of you together, then give him copies, some in frames. Note the small things he uses daily, and replace the ones he has with beautiful gifts from you: things like a pen, a coffee cup, silk underwear, a key case, a wallet, even a mouse pad for his computer. You will soon become an omni-presence in his life.

Let him know that you will not be around forever. In conversations that are light and non-threatening, let him know that your past relationships usually die out after about six months, or whatever the number may be. By then you can tell if a man is going to be right for you or not, and you're in the habit of moving on. As your relationship progresses, you can drop hints like, "Can you believe we've been seeing each other for three months already? Most men start the down-hill slide from here, but I think you're doing pretty well." As the time limit you've set for yourself approaches, start acting restless.

Develop an acute sense of timing. Timing can be everything, my dear. When you're in the throes of passion, and it's all you can do to keep from racing to the bedroom, say some-thing like, "If we were married right now I would absolutely *devour* you!" Those kinds of lines have garnered me six on-the-spot proposals from wealthy men. Try to discern exactly which words would work best at which moment, and use them mercilessly.

Distance yourself from those he's had bad experiences with. Your millionaire might still be reeling from a bad relationship, and be working under the assumption that "all women are alike." Find out about his failed relationships. (He'll probably be very willing to talk about them.) Then subtly, at other times, point out the differences between yourself and those other women, or your current relationship and the ones he had with them. Say things like, "Well, baby, you know that when you call and I'm not home at night, I'm definitely not out dancing in the clubs." Or, "We have such an honest and open relationship. I don't think there's anything I wouldn't tell you if you asked." He will make the favorable comparisons in his mind.

Assure him of what your answer would be if he were to propose. Millionaires absolutely despise failure and rejection. If you've done too good a job of convincing him that you're not desperate, he might simply be afraid to ask you. Through subtle hints, erase all doubts as to what your answer would be.

Show him good examples of happy marriages. The institution itself might scare him, especially if he's had bad experiences with it in the past. If you have a sibling or a close friend with a happy marriage, try to associate with them often. I like to take my prospective men home to my sister's beautiful house. My brother-in-law is great, their children are unsurpassed, and I can't tell you how many men have come away saying, "I wouldn't mind having a family like theirs."

Make sure his life is better when you're around than when you're not. Try to make his life richer and fuller by bringing interesting new things into it—ideas, foods, music, people, poetry, etc. Call the beautiful things around him to his attention. Point out a gorgeous sunset as he's hurrying to an appointment. Keep the nagging to a minimum, and don't accost him with your woes when you first see him. Discover what makes him happy, and make sure it's magnified when you're around.

If your true love has a hard time making decisions, propose to him. Be careful with this one, though. Many men like to feel as if they're the hunters and you are the game to be bagged. But some are weary of the whole process. One of the most eligible millionaires I know, in his late 30s and never married, often tells me, "You know, L.A., if some woman I enjoyed and respected asked me to marry her one day, I'd do it. I really would. It would be nice just to finally make the leap." This man would make an excellent husband, too.

THE UP AND UP ON THE PRENUP

You've done so well and come so far! He's proposed and you've accepted. Don't let a silly little thing like a spat over the prenuptial agreement keep you from the alter. Let's see if you know how to handle it. The proper response when your millionaire brings the subject up is to say:

A. How could you even dream of asking me to sign something like that? Don't you trust me? Don't you believe in our relationship?

B. Of course, darling, I'll do anything you say. Just show me where to sign!

C. None of the above.

Although A and B are by far the most common responses, C is your correct answer. You should not react emotionally to the prenuptial agreement. It is a document of practicality, and you really wouldn't want a millionaire who proved to be impractical, would you?

Where there's a millionaire, there's a prenuptial. It comes with the turf. Wealthy men who married years ago, when prenuptials weren't as common, and had to give up half of everything they owned to their ex-wives, are particularly conscious of this. If your millionaire has been married more than once, you might have a previous prenuptial agreement to thank for the fact that he's still a millionaire.

It may not be the most romantic thing in the world to discuss the possibility that your marriage could end before you do, but the simple fact of the matter is that nearly 50 percent of the marriages in the U.S. end in divorce. That means you have a 50-50 chance of making your marriage work. Of course almost everyone who says "I do" believes that they will be in the successful 50 percent, but half of them won't. Your chances of splitting up are just as great as your chances of staying together, so preparing for either option is not unwise.

Besides, you can make the prenuptial agreement work for you. The basic document states that if the marriage ends, what you brought into the marriage is yours, what he brought in is his, and any increase during the time of your marriage is split 50-50.

The prenuptial agreement cannot limit the child support of the children you have together, because that would involve individuals who were not around to sign the document. It can, however, limit alimony which must be, according to the law, enough to keep you above the poverty level and off welfare.

This can work to your advantage. If the document you sign limits alimony, make sure it's enough to support you in the manner to which the millionaire has helped you become accustomed. Chances are it will be much more than what you were making before you married him, or than you would be making on your own, so there's really nothing to complain about, unless you're extremely greedy.

Another thing the document might try to limit is your claim to your millionaire's increase after the marriage. It might keep you from sharing family funds, or it might specify that what you make while you're married will be yours, and what he makes will be his. You'll want to have a lawyer go over this point with you. If you're planning on staying home and taking care of the kids while he's out working, signing an agreement like that could keep you from getting what you're entitled to, and you should question it.

A prenuptial agreement can also help you avoid an estate battle with children from a previous marriage in the event of your millionaire's death. Make sure your document specifies how the estate will be divided, and use this as an excuse to talk to him about updating his will. There have actually been quite a few instances where a millionaire has finally found the love of his life in his latter years, and died shortly after the marriage. His other heirs, who resented the last marriage anyway, fought like rabid tigers to keep the new wife from getting her due. You must protect yourself from this.

If you perceive that your millionaire might balk at these posthumous suggestions and get the impression that you're eager for his demise, you can soften things by assuring him that you will make the same stipulations about your own property. You will happily sign a contract stating that he will inherit your wealth when you die, and that he will be the beneficiary of your life insurance policy. Your financial worth might not be even close to his, but he will be touched by your gesture.

You also might want to go for a few frills in your prenuptial agreement. Do you have any children you want him to adopt? This, along with inheritance and provisions for their support if the marriage ends, can be covered. And then there is medical and disability insurance coverage. It is practical to ensure that he will pay all the premiums, even if your marriage breaks up.

Once again, I must stress that all these negotiations be kept businesslike and unemotional. If you sense that your millionaire is becoming irritated, back off and try to soothe him. If you yourself are getting frustrated, take an emotion break as well. A close friend of mine whose family is worth billions chuckled as he told me about signing the prenuptial with his bride-to-be. "She's a sharp one, she is. She had her attorney go over the whole thing, and added a few stipulations of her own. Nothing gets by this one. She's going to be a great wife!"

You see, prenuptials are not really as prickly as they sound. I once quite surprised the millionaire I was getting serious with when he attempted to discern my feelings on the prenuptial agreement. "Oh, I believe it's essential for me to protect my assets!" I said enthusiastically. "I wouldn't dream of getting married without having my fiancé sign a legal document!" Comparing my assets to his, my millionaire had to laugh. But he realized I was serious about it.

The proper response when a millionaire questions you about prenuptial agreements is:

D. Of course. Let's draw one up, and I'll have my attorney take a look at it.

ONE LAST TRUTH

There you have it, darling. All that remains is for you to gaze at your millionaire lovingly and say, "I do." However, if you never get to this point with a wealthy man, don't be too depressed. Your life is not over, nor will you necessarily have to settle for second best.

Remember, you've been dating millionaires partially for the sake of experience, partially for the sake of comparison. As I mentioned at the beginning of this book, you might take a taste of the rich cream, and then find that you prefer the wholesomeness of skim milk. In all my varied experiences with dating millionaires, there is one truth that has emerged far above the rest:

It isn't what a man *has* that satisfies me. It's what a man is. By the time you finish with this book, you should realize this too. Good luck, and happy hunting.

EPILOGUE

Congratulations! You've finished this volume and are well on your way to happily snaring a wealth of rich men. Now I have one last suggestion. Hide this book. You might want to save it for future reference, but don't let the millionaires catch you reading it. It would devastate them to discover that you're using a published formula for capturing them. They like to think of themselves as being beyond manipulation or predictability, and you, of course, must support this delusion. Hide the book—maybe under your bed—right now. Good luck!

Marie Papillon has been hailed as *the* authority on love and romance. All over the world, men and women have learned her secrets of amour with fantastic results. Now, in her phenomenal bestselling book, she reveals:

- How, where and even when to meet that special someone—from walking the dog to working out to hosting a "blind date" party

- How to become an irresistible flirt—mastering verbal and non-verbal techniques...from making eye contact to talking on the phone to computer flirting!

- Tips for rekindling passion—from planning romantic menus for "theme evenings" to sending a bouquet of balloons and other creative ideas!

- Helpful hints for romance on a budget

- And much more!

A Million & One Love Strategies

♥ Marie Papillon ♥

A MILLION AND ONE LOVE STRATEGIES
Marie Papillon
_____ 95466-2 $5.99 U.S./$6.99 CAN.